RACE
TO
INCARCERATE

MARC MAUER

The Sentencing Project

THE NEW PRESS   NEW YORK

Library of Congress Cataloging-in-Publication Data

Mauer, Marc.
    Race to incarcerate / Marc Mauer & The Sentencing Project.
        p.   cm.
    Includes bibliographical references and index.
    ISBN 1-56584-429-7 (pbk.)
       1. Criminal justice, Administration of — United States.   2. Prison
sentences — United States.   3. Imprisonment — United States.   4. Crime
prevention — United States.   5. Discrimination in criminal justice
administration — United States.   I. Sentencing Project (U.S.)
II. Title.
HV9950.M32   1999
364.6'0973 — dc21   98-46750
                                                         CIP

Parts of Chapter 4 previously appeared in a different version in *Social Justice: A Journal of Crime, Conflict, and World Order*, Fall 1994; reprinted with permission.

Published in the United States by The New Press, New York
Distributed by W. W. Norton & Company, Inc., New York

The New Press was established in 1990 as a not-for-profit alternative to the large, commercial publishing houses currently dominating the book publishing industry. The New Press operates in the public interest rather than for private gain, and is committed to publishing, in innovative ways, works of educational, cultural, and community value that might not be considered sufficiently profitable. The New Press's editorial offices are located at the City University of New York.

Printed in the United States of America

9 8 7 6 5 4 3 2 1

To Barbara, Joanna and Daniel

—Contents

RACE

TO

INCARCERATE

Acknowledgments

The idea for this book originated with Joe Wood, my editor at The New Press. He cleverly convinced me that much of the book was already written in my head and all I had to do was to set it down on paper. It turned out to be not quite that simple, but I'm grateful for the opportunity he provided and for his sharp editorial guidance throughout the process.

This book in large part reflects my work and experiences with The Sentencing Project over the past decade. One could not ask for a more congenial and encouraging environment in which to pursue ideas and issues. Malcolm Young provided initial encouragement to take on this project and has served throughout as a fine editor, source of intellectual support, and friend. Beth Carter helped me track down numerous references and relevant articles, Pat Garavito provided masterful word-processing and editorial skills, Gayle Hebron ensured that all our administrative bases were covered in a timely fashion, and Jodie Minor was always eager to aid in the production process.

The work of The Sentencing Project would not have been possible through these years without the strong backing of private funding sources that were willing to support a small nonprofit organization in its efforts to take on the challenging task of advocating for change in the nation's crime policies. For their foresight and encouragement, many thanks in particular to the Annie E. Casey Foundation, the Center on Crime, Communities and Culture of the Open Society Institute, the Edna McConnell Clark Foundation, the John D. and Catherine T. MacArthur Foundation, and the Public Welfare Foundation.

Many friends and colleagues in the field have been most gracious and giving of their time in helping with this project. Jerry McElroy read the entire manuscript and provided all the insightful analyses I have come to expect of him. Others who reviewed various chapters and helped to critique and sharpen my arguments were Meda Chesney-Lind, Angela Jordan Davis, Steve Jonas, and Jolanta Juszkiewicz. Special thanks to Bill Sabol, not only for reviewing some of these chapters but also for providing keen observations over the years on a variety of projects. My research was also substantially aided by Pam Hollenhorst, who efficiently and skillfully helped to shape the issues for Chapter 9, and by Ted Ashby, who tracked down a variety of bibliographical sources. Other friends aided in my search for resources, obscure references, and historical recollections. Thanks in this regard to Rob Allen, Carol Bergman, Scott Christianson, Walter Dickey, Dick Dieter, Jenni Gainsborough, Judy Greene, Russ Immarigeon, Naneen Karraker, Jan Marinnisen, Bill Nagel, and Dick Scobie for their assistance in this and many other ways over the years. My special appreciation as well to Gil Kline, media consultant to The Sentencing Project, for his astute observations and accomplishments over the years on our public policy projects, and to Michael Castleman, for his guidance on the world of publishing.

Any kind of writing, of course, is the product of one's environment and experiences. I could not have been more fortunate in this regard. Warm thanks to my mother, Mildred Mauer, and my brother, Michael Mauer, for everything they've given me through the years and for sharing my commitment to social justice. And, on the home front, my wife, Barbara Francisco, and my children, Joanna and Daniel, put up with many dinnertime reports regarding progress on "the book" and have been my daily sources of inspiration.

Preface

In the course of writing this book, I received a call requesting research assistance. My caller wanted to know how many inmates were in the prison systems of a number of different nations in order to determine the total size of the "market." The caller turned out to be a researcher for an investment firm, and the "market" represented the potential for global investment and expansion of privately built and operated prisons. Now that products and profits can be made anywhere around the world, apparently there is no reason for American corporations to confine their thinking about the profitability of crime control to the borders of the United States.

At various times in history, prisoners have been thought of as sinners, deviants, or members of an oppressed class. As we approach the twenty-first century, they have now become mere commodities in the eyes of global entrepreneurs.

While the new century brings with it promises of horizon-expanding technology, it is ironic that the institution of the prison, an invention of the eighteenth century, is not only still with us but expanding at a rapid rate. Those in the field of criminal justice who seek to develop creative approaches to involving communities in crime prevention must now compete with proposals to reinstate chain gangs and other relics of a time we had thought was past.

This book tries to assess how U. S. society has come to rely on the use of imprisonment to an extent that was entirely unforeseen and even unimaginable just thirty years ago. How is it that our national approach to solving the problem of crime has come to rely so dramatically on the bricks and mortar of the prison at the expense of other responses that would be both more humane and more effective?

For my friends and colleagues who toil in the nation's prisons and jails each day, let me say at the outset that this is a book about criminal justice policy, not the individuals charged with implementing that policy. Indeed, many of the corrections officials and prison wardens who run these institutions are dedicated professionals who share a vision of a more humane and effective system of justice, and who often labor in extremely trying circumstances.

This book may be interpreted as a critique of the "tough on crime" movement that has characterized the nation's approach to crime and criminal justice for more than a quarter century. It does present a challenge to that approach, in fact, but only a willful misinterpretation could categorize it as being unconcerned about crime. If we hope to work our way toward a more effective approach to crime and violence, it is incumbent upon us to look at where we've been and to explore where we might go from here. One would hope that in our national debate on crime we could at least all agree that what is being discussed are competing policy proposals and visions of a safer society. This book offers a contribution to that discussion.

1—Introduction—
The Race to Incarcerate

We're on a new higher plateau of crime, which means a new, higher and,
I think, permanent prison population. It is very hard for a free society to
figure out how effectively to deal with crime rates other than by impris-
onment.
                                                            —James Q. Wilson[1]

What an interesting populace we have. Nobody seems at all worried by
the fact that we have the largest prison population and that it consists
preponderantly of young blacks, a whole generation in jail.
                                                            —Murray Kempton[2]

In January 1998, the Justice Department issued its semian-
nual report on prison populations in the United States, not-
ing that there had been a five percent rise in the previous
twelve months. Newspapers dutifully reported the story, just as
they had similar rises the year before and the year before that. In
fact, by now the story was a quarter century old, with the national prison population having risen nearly 500 percent since
1972, far greater than the 28 percent rise in the national population during that time. In the ten-year period beginning in 1985,
federal and state governments had opened a new prison a week
to cope with the flood of prisoners. The nearly 1.2 million inmates in the nation's prisons was almost six times greater than
prior to the inception of the prison-building boom and represented a societal use of incarceration that was virtually unique
by world standards. The scale of imprisonment had come a long
way since the birth of the institution.

Two hundred years ago, Quakers and other reformers in
Pennsylvania had developed the institution of the penitentiary,
an experiment in molding human behavior that was befitting of
other innovations in the new democracy of the United States.
Derived from the concept of "penitence," the new institution

emphasized having sinners engage in hard labor and reflect upon the errors of their ways.

Prior to this, the preferred methods of responding to criminal behavior in both the European nations of the old world and in the American colonies did not include institutions. The jails that existed in Europe and the U.S. served primarily to detain defendants who were awaiting trial and debtors who had not fulfilled their obligations, and they were not places of punishment for felons.

After a defendant was convicted of an offense, various measures were employed with the goal of deterring the individual from engaging in antisocial behavior in the future. Deviant behavior was viewed not as reflecting a flaw in society but, rather, as sinful and pervasive in society. Those who had offended were generally subjected to relatively swift and severe sanctions, which often varied depending on one's status in the community. For persons of some means who had committed relatively minor offenses, fines were frequently imposed as punishment. Lower-status persons convicted of offenses—servants, apprentices, slaves, and laborers—were usually subjected to the stocks or public whippings. The death penalty was an option in cases as serious as murder, but also for lesser offenses, such as third-time thievery. The use of capital punishment, though, was far less frequent in the colonies than in England. Offenders in the colonies who were not from the immediate community, and sometimes repeat offenders, were generally subject to banishment.

Much of the rationale for these various punishments can be found in the nature of the colonial society. In an environment where communities were relatively small and their inhabitants well known to each other, public approbation and embarrassment was seen as capable of shaming the offender into desisting from continued illegal activities. Wandering rogues who went from town to town committing crimes were usually banished. Moreover, in a society where labor was in short supply, benefits to the community were derived from punishments that, being swift and certain, did not unduly affect the laboring capacity of the community.

After the Revolution, though, new ways of thinking about crime and punishment began to emerge. In 1787, influential Quakers and other leaders in Pennsylvania, led by Dr. Benjamin Rush, organized the Philadelphia Society for Alleviating the Miseries of Public Prisons.[3] A growing sentiment that the death penalty and other corporal punishments were barbaric eventually led to restrictions or elimination of capital punishment in the new states.

But if the death penalty was to be eliminated, or its use greatly reduced, how would serious offenders be punished? These and other issues were considered by the nation's leaders. Out of these deliberations came the notion of the prison as a new form of punishment and deterrence for both capital and noncapital offenders.

The initial experiment in confining convicted offenders took place in 1790: it involved converting sixteen cells at Philadelphia's Walnut Street Jail into housing for felons. This was later replaced and expanded upon at the Eastern State Penitentiary in 1829, which remained in use until 1970. The Pennsylvania penitentiary model was based on imprisoning offenders in solitary confinement and occupying them with labor and Bible study in their cells; those who were unable to read were aided by outside volunteers.

Ironically, and in retrospect quite tellingly, the first inmate admitted to the Eastern State Penitentiary was a "light skinned Negro in excellent health," described by an observer as "one who was born of a degraded and depressed race, and had never experienced anything but indifference and harshness."[4] Two centuries later, the confluence of issues of race and class with the prison system have become a fundamental feature of the national landscape.

Variations on the penitentiary model used the basic format of confining offenders to solitary cells, but exposing them to a congregate work environment. This approach was pioneered in the

1820s by the "Auburn model" in New York State, which required inmates to engage in work during the day; prisoners were prohibited from talking or even exchanging glances. Fierce debates raged at the time regarding the efficacy of the competing Pennsylvania and New York models in controlling crime. However, common to both systems was the belief that the less communication offenders had with each other, the less opportunity there would be to engage in criminal plotting or to reinforce each other's negative orientation.

By the mid-1800s, changes in the makeup of American society—no longer a relatively sparsely populated collection of small towns and cities—led to a new consensus regarding how best to respond to criminal behavior. The demographic and economic growth of the nation had spawned increasing concern about antisocial behavior and ways of maintaining order in an increasingly fluid society. Out of this came a growing consensus among leaders of the day regarding the need for an institutional response to potential disorder.

Looking back on two centuries of the prison in America, what is particularly remarkable is how little the institutional model has changed since the nineteenth century. While the philosophical orientation and stated goals of the prison have fluctuated, the basic concept of imprisoning people in cages remains the central feature of the system.

It is a bit jarring, of course, to speak of "caging" human beings, since we normally prefer to use this term for animals and to conjure up fond feelings for our favorite zoo (although our common feelings about the constraints placed on animals in cages have also changed markedly in recent years). But whether we call them "cells," or "housing units," or any other new name, it is difficult to deny that the basic reality of the system is that of the cage.

To place the permanence of the model in perspective, we need only consider how other institutions and professions have evolved over these past two hundred years. In transportation, we have moved from the horse and buggy to the steam engine, the automobile, and now, ventures deep into the solar system. In medicine, healing methods based on limited scientific expertise have been eclipsed by such remarkably sophisticated measures as open heart surgery and even the possibility of cloning human beings. Understandings of human behavior likewise have been dramatically altered by the advances of psychotherapy, along with a host of twentieth-century theories. Yet the prison cell endures after two centuries.

This is not to say that prison systems are necessarily operated in an eighteenth-century fashion, or that change is never instituted. Despite the re-introduction of chain gangs, old-styled convict uniforms, and other methods of humiliation, there still remain many corrections administrators who take pride in their work and are earnest advocates for humane conditions of confinement. Indeed, in some newer prisons, the cage itself has been replaced by locked rooms in a dormitory-like setting. Nevertheless, the themes of confinement and isolation remain central to the model of the prison.

The way a society deals with offending behavior is first conditioned on how that behavior is defined, a value that evolves over time and across cultures. Within the United States, alcohol production was prohibited in the 1930s, but has been permitted for the most part during all other periods. Even among more serious offenses, both cultural and situational relevance determine societal responses. Killing a person, for example, is clearly outlawed in daily life, but permitted by all nations in times of war. State-sanctioned killings in the form of the death penalty are permitted in such nations as the United States, China, and Iran, but prohibited in most industrialized nations and many developing nations as well.

Prisons and the entire apparatus of a criminal justice system represent a response to offending behaviors. The system is viewed as a means of retribution and problem-solving, that of responding to persons and behaviors we find unacceptable. But, most critically, the system itself is premised on being a *reactive* model and a *punitive* system—that is, the criminal justice system comes into play only after a crime has been committed. At that point, the victim may call 911, the police will investigate, the prosecutor brings charges, and a judge imposes a sentence if there is a conviction. Each of these actions are appropriate in and of themselves, but our familiarity with them tends to mask any consideration of the underlying approach suggested by this model.

By identifying certain persons or groups of people as "criminals," a punitive model of responding to social problems is made to appear almost inevitable. However, this model of problem-solving is hardly preordained. Families and communities regularly employ a host of services and resources to encourage what are believed to be appropriate behaviors and to discourage antisocial behaviors. In the vast majority of cases, these approaches are pro-active ones. Thus, we establish schools to educate our children, we form religious bodies to communicate values, and we act as parents to transmit styles of behavior that we regard as ethical or beneficial.

In many communities, applying these approaches results in an environment with well-functioning members that, in crime terms, is considered "safe." But when we think of a community that is "safe," is it one with the most police or the most frequent use of the death penalty? Of course not. Rather, it is one with clean, well-lit streets, open businesses, and little fear. These often happen to be communities with high income levels, strong families and community resources, and ones that both value their members and have the means by which to assure that most of them will do well in society.

In contrast, other communities become defined as "bad" or "unsafe," and are ones that contain inordinate numbers of "criminals." At this point, a rational society would be challenged to develop an approach to ensure more safety for these communities. One approach might be to provide the community with more resources, or to facilitate the ability of its members to assert more control over the offending behaviors. Increasingly, though, the model of choice has been the use of the criminal justice system and its punitive orientation. Whether intended or not, this approach is intimately connected with perceptions of race and class. So, while public support may be forthcoming for "tough" penalties and the politicians who propose them, when it is one of our own who gets into trouble, we seem to view the problem very differently.

In recent years, we have seen this distinction played out most directly in the national approach to drug abuse. Millions of middle-class families have experienced the pain of seeing a loved one succumb to drug abuse or addiction. Their response, by and large, is one that recognizes this as a social problem for which social interventions are necessary. Identifying a high-quality treatment program, with the aid of private insurance, becomes the preferred response to the problem.

In contrast, for nearly two decades the nation has been engaged in a very different "war on drugs" to respond to drug abuse and its associated ills among low-income and minority families. Treatment programs are likely to be in short supply, so the problem of abuse is much more likely to fester and eventually result in actions that will define it as a criminal justice problem.

None of this should suggest, of course, that crime is not a problem of serious concern, or that minority communities are not particularly affected by dramatically high rates of violence. In fact, for many years minority communities have bemoaned the lack of police attention to their concerns as well as complained of police harassment. A complex set of factors, though, fueled in large part by a haze of media images and political soundbites, has almost inured us to any approaches to dealing with these problems other than punitive criminal justice models. And, while we continue to suffer from crime rates that are higher than many can remember from the 1950s, a quarter century of "tough" policies has failed to provide sufficient safety or to substantially reduce the fear of crime.

Some observers of these developments have concluded that the crime and criminal justice policies of the present era represent a conspiratorial assault on minority communities. To believe this, though, negates the actual progress that has been made in securing minority representation in leadership positions within the justice system. Progress in this regard is still relatively modest in many jurisdictions, but the past twenty years have indeed witnessed a substantial increase in the number of black and Hispanic police chiefs, judges, corrections officials, and others in positions of authority.

It is more productive to examine the stated and unstated assumptions that have guided criminal justice policy, as well as the choices not presented or chosen. A black judge confronted with indigent drug addicts and inadequate treatment resources is in as difficult a position at sentencing as a white judge: both are daily confronted with the consequences of broader policy decisions that have disinvested in communities and implicitly chosen a reactive and punitive response to broad social problems, rather than a pro-active and constructive one.

The essentially reactive nature of the criminal justice model has been of concern to many, both in terms of its efficacy in responding to the problem of crime and in terms of establishing a two-tiered system of community problem-solving. Indeed, throughout the history of the use of imprisonment in the United States, there have been critiques of the model, organized efforts at reform, and challenges to the prevailing wisdom. As early as the 1840s, Charles Dickens bemoaned the model he witnessed in Philadelphia: "Those who devised this system . . . and those benevolent gentlemen who carry it into execution do not know what . . . they are doing." On the nature of the institution, he concluded that "I hold this slow and daily tampering with the mysteries of the brain, to be immeasurably worse than any torture of the body."[5]

In recent times, the social upheavals of the 1960s produced a prison reform movement both within the prisons and among outside supporters. Often led or influenced by black Muslims within the institutions, the movement raised a broad critique of the prison system itself, the definition of crime, and the coercive power of the state. While elements of this critique have always been present, events of the past quarter century have now elevated its significance in profound ways. During this period, public policy in the United States has resulted in what can only be termed a second wave of the great "experiment" in the use of incarceration as a means of controlling crime. As we shall see, a complex set of social and political developments have produced a wave of building and filling prisons virtually unprecedented in human history. Beginning with a prison population of just under 200,000 in 1972, the number of inmates in U.S. prisons has increased by nearly one million, rising to almost 1.2 million by 1997. Along with the more than one half million inmates in local jails either awaiting trial or serving short sentences, a remarkable total of 1.7 million Americans are now behind bars.

These figures take on more meaning in comparison with other nations in the industrialized world. The U.S. rate of incarceration per capita now dwarfs that of almost all such nations: our nation locks up offenders at a rate six to ten times that of most comparable countries. Ironically, the United States now competes only with Russia for the dubious distinction of maintaining the world lead in the rate at which its citizens are locked up. Although the Cold War has ended and the arms race is essentially over, these two nations with vastly different economies and social conditions now are engaged in a race to incarcerate.

Like the arms race, the race to incarcerate has a set of consequences for society that have generally been examined only in the most shallow of ways. Moreover, as we approach the new millennium, the nature and meaning of incarceration in the United States has changed in a variety of profound ways with far-reaching implications.

First among these is the virtual institutionalization of a societal commitment to the use of a massive prison system. More than half of the prisons in use today have been constructed in the last twenty years. These prisons can be expected to endure and imprison for at least fifty years, virtually guaranteeing a national commitment to a high rate of incarceration. The growth of the system itself serves to create a set of institutionalized lobbying forces that perpetuate a societal commitment to imprisonment through the expansion of vested economic interests. The more than 600,000 prison and jail guards, administrators, service workers, and other personnel represent a potentially powerful political opposition to any scaling-down of the system. One need only recall the fierce opposition to the closing of military bases in recent year to see how these forces will function over time.

Prisons as sources of economic growth have also become vital to the development strategy of many small rural communities that have lost jobs in recent years but hold the lure of cheap land and a ready workforce. Communities that once organized against the siting of new prisons now beg state officials to construct new institutions in their backyards.

Add to this the rapidly expanding prison privatization movement focused on the "bottom line" of profiting from imprisonment. In the words of one industry call to potential investors, "While arrests and convictions are steadily on the rise, profits are to be made—*profits from crime*. Get in on the ground floor of this booming industry now."[6]

Nevertheless, it is not as if there are no models to guide us in making the transition toward less use of incarceration. The de-institutionalization of the mental health system, which began in the 1960s, was hardly an unqualified success, due primarily to the failure to enhance sufficiently community-based services; yet, it remains a model that demonstrates the possibility of embracing new approaches that challenge conventional wisdom.

Prison reformers of the 1960s and 1970s often maintained a cautious optimism that a de-institutionalization movement in corrections would follow that of the mental health system. Their reasoning was that similar critiques could be made of both types of systems, but that greater public empathy for mental patients than criminal offenders inevitably would result in an easier transition for the mental health model. With the benefit of hindsight, we can now see that this faith was quite misplaced.

The near-permanent status of the massive state of imprisonment is evidenced despite the expressed concern over the "crisis" of prison overcrowding which has accompanied public policy discussion and media accounts of these issues. Pleas have been made that funding for an expanded prison system will divert resources from other public spending, and that prison capacity cannot be expanded quickly enough to accommodate a steadily growing number of inmates.

After a quarter century of prison growth, though, it is now apparent that while some corrections officials may feel the impact of an expanding system and overcrowding, in fact there is really no longer a "crisis" mentality in many regards. Rather, vastly expanded expenditures on corrections system are now considered the norm, and in fact, represent the largest growth area of state budgets. Virtually every state has engaged in a significant if not massive prison construction program over the past two decades, financed through general funds, bonds, and more recently, public–private venture arrangements. While prisons in most states still remain overcrowded, the level of overcrowding has not changed appreciably since 1990, which demonstrates that state and the federal governments have been quite willing to construct new institutions in response to growing demand. Finally, while there still remains some discussion regarding the need to refrain from unlimited growth in the system, any consideration of an actual reduction in the absolute size of the prison population is virtually absent from public policy discussion.

Contributing to the establishment of this permanent state of mass incarceration is the impact of falling crime rates of the 1990s. For proponents of expanded imprisonment, a falling rate of crime is virtually all the proof needed to justify an expensive and inherently coercive institution: if imprisonment goes up and crime rates go down, they argue, the correlation between these two must be obvious. As we shall see later, this "relationship" is far from clear and certainly not one that should justify such a commitment of resources. Nonetheless, at a time when political leaders can boast of their "success" in reducing crime rates, any criticism of the prison state has difficulty gaining attention.

It is hard to imagine that this complacency would exist if the more than a million and a half prisoners were the sons and daughters of the white middle class. However, as the image of the criminal as an urban black male has hardened into public consciousness, so too, has support for punitive approaches to social problems been enhanced. Little talk is heard of the feasibility of expanded employment or educational opportunities as a means of crime prevention: welfare "reform" gains a bipartisan political consensus, despite dire predictions of large increases in child poverty, and policymaker acceptance of a "permanent underclass" proceeds apace. In a changed economy with less demand for the labor of many unskilled workers, imprisonment begins to be seen as an appropriate, if unfortunate, outcome.

While the impact of incarceration on individuals can be quantified to a certain extent, the wide-ranging effects of the race to incarcerate on African American communities in particular is a phenomenon that is only beginning to be investigated. What does it mean to a community, for example, to know that three out of ten boys growing up will spend time in prison? What does it do to the fabric of the family and community to have such a substantial proportion of its young men enmeshed in the criminal justice system? What images and values are communicated to young people who see the prisoner as the most prominent or pervasive role model in the community? What is the effect on a community's political influence when one quarter of the black men in some states cannot vote as a result of a felony conviction? Surely these are not healthy developments.

Moreover, we have entered an era of technology and communications in which developments in crime policy in the United States take on an increasingly global influence. While the U.S. hegemony over world economies and culture has long been observed and often decried, there are now ominous signs that the incarceration models and mentality so pervasive in this country are affecting social policy abroad as well.

This trend is probably most obvious in England, where Michael Howard, the former Home Secretary of John Major's Conservative government in the mid-1990s, embraced many of the "get tough" policies developed in the United States. Breaking with a historic British tradition of granting broad discretion and independence to the judiciary, Howard proposed the adoption of mandatory sentences, boot camps, "supermax" high control prisons, and other U.S. innovations. This was accompanied by U.S. "photo-op" visits by Howard to such institutions as the Florence, Colorado, federal "supermax" prison, considered the ultimate form of institutional control, a high-tech operation with almost complete isolation of inmates from each other and the outside world.

The government's initiatives might have been dismissed as merely pandering to a conservative constituency had they not represented such a sharp break with the recent past of the Conservative government. Under the previous leadership of Margaret Thatcher, the government had instituted the 1991 Criminal Justice Act, which essentially recognized the limited impact of incarceration on crime and called for a halt in the growth of the prison system. Developed from a cost-efficiency standpoint, the policy had been promoted as fiscally conservative and responsible.

These developments are not confined to England, though. With worldwide access to media ranging from CNN to the internet, policymakers and the public are now virtually instantaneously exposed to social changes in the United States. In recent years, we have therefore seen such legislative proposals as a "three strikes and you're out" policy in the Czech Republic based on televised reports from California. More sinister is the broad reach of the American prison privatization movement; U.S. private prison companies are winning contracts from Australia to eastern Europe. Policies that imprison ever-larger numbers of young African American males in the United States are also likely to result, at least indirectly, in greater incarceration of immigrants in Norway or minority populations in France.

Thus, there is now an even greater obligation on the part of policymakers and the public in the United States to consider their actions and impact not only on the domestic "underclass" but on democratic rights and traditions internationally. It is these issues and analyses that we shall explore in this volume.

NOTES

1. Interview in *Criminal Justice Matters* (Autumn 1996), p. 4.
2. Quoted in Alfred Kazin, "Missing Murray Kempton," *New York Times Book Review*, 30 Nov. 1997, p. 35.
3. Although prisons as institutions of punishment had not yet emerged in the new nation, jails for debtors and defendants awaiting trial had previously existed.
4. Negley K. Teeters and John D. Shearer, *The Prison at Philadelphia, Cherry Hill; The Separate System of Prison Discipline, 1829–1913* (New York: Columbia University Press, 1957), p. 84.
5. Charles Dickens, *American Notes* (1842; Penguin ed., 1972), p. 146, as cited in Lawrence M. Friedman, *Crime and Punishment in American History* (New York: Basic Books, 1993), p. 80.
6. Jennifer L. Berk, World Research Group, conference invitation letter, December 1996.

2—The Incarceration "Experiment"

In 1971, David Rothman, one of the leading historians of the birth of the penitentiary, closed his highly regarded work, *The Discovery of the Asylum*, with these words: ". . . we have been gradually escaping from institutional responses and one can foresee the period when incarceration will be used *still more rarely* than it is today."[1]

The value of Rothman's contributions to this field of scholarship should not be diminished by this unfortunate prediction, but rarely has such a gaze into the future proven to be so wide off the mark as this one.

The prediction didn't seem so wrong at the time. Three years after Rothman's book appeared, Jan Marinissen of the American Friends Service Committee approached the Unitarian Universalist Service Committee (UUSC) with a bold idea for a new campaign. Marinissen suggested the formation of an organization dedicated to working for a moratorium on all new prison construction. The purpose of such a moratorium would be to permit time for a range of appropriate alternatives to incarceration to be developed which could aid in reducing the need for new prison space.

Marinissen's proposal was bold, but hardly out of the mainstream of much leading criminal justice thinking of the day. Despite political winds that were developing a "law and order" approach to crime, many professionals and academics were headed in a very different direction. In 1972, the National Council on Crime and Delinquency, a venerable reform organization, had passed a policy statement calling for a halt to institutional construction. The following year, the National Advisory Commission on Criminal Justice Standards and Goals issued a recommendation that "no new institutions for adults should be built and existing institutions for juveniles should be closed,"[2] and concluded that "the prison, the reformatory, and the jail have achieved only a shocking record of failure. There is over-whelming evidence that these institutions create crime rather than prevent it."[3]

The UUSC was enthusiastic about the moratorium idea, and proceeded to provide funding and to establish a Washington-based organization, the National Moratorium on Prison Construction, in 1975. The organization quickly became a significant focal point for prison reformers and activists, and engaged a national network of state-based campaigns and affiliates. From its Washington base, the Moratorium garnered a fair amount of media attention along with maintaining a presence on Capitol Hill until the mid-1980s. Its appeals for a prison moratorium were based on a combination of arguments—the cost of building prisons was too high, alternatives to incarceration were more appropriate for many offenders, and justice required that prison only be used as a last resort.

The viewpoint of the moratorium effort was both hopelessly naive and startlingly prescient. In retrospect, what is perhaps most remarkable about its inception was the context of imprisonment in the United States at that time. In 1972, federal and state prisons held 196,000 inmates, yielding an incarceration rate of 93 per 100,000 population. In addition, approximately 130,000 inmates were being held in local jails, thus resulting in an overall rate of incarceration of about 160 per 100,000 population, or one of every 625 Americans.[4] This rate of incarceration is a level so low that it is not even in the realm of possibility for the 1990s, but for moratorium supporters, this magnitude of imprisonment was egregiously high.

Supporters of the moratorium effort can be forgiven for being so naive, since the prison expansion that was about to take place was virtually unprecedented in human history. In fact, if one examines the 45-year period leading up to the 1970s, what is most notable is the remarkable stability of the rate of incarceration, averaging about 110 per 100,000 (excluding the jail population). As we can see in Figure 2-1, some fluctuations certainly are evident during this period. Rates of incarceration rose dur-

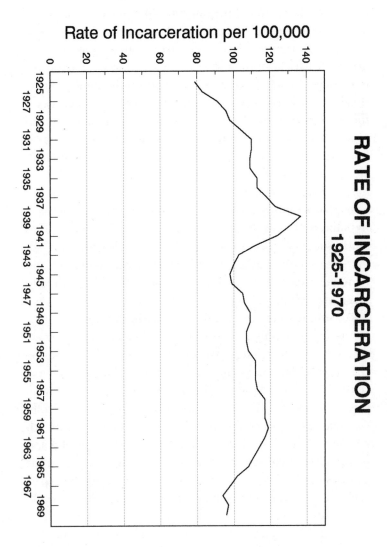

Figure 2-1
Rate of Incarceration, 1925–1970

Source: Bureau of Justice Statistics, *Sourcebook of Criminal Justice Statistics,* 1996, U.S. Department of Justice, Washington, D.C., 1997

ing the Depression, perhaps because more crimes were being committed as a result of the difficult economic circumstances. Following this period, the number of inmates fell during World War II for two reasons. First, many of the young men who might otherwise have been committing crimes leading to their imprisonment were instead overseas fighting for their country. Anecdotal evidence also suggests that the pressing need for bodies in the military may have influenced criminal justice policy and practice: a nation desperate to turn its citizens into soldiers is less likely to resort to incarceration if a milder punishment, along with enlistment in the army, will suffice.

The relative stability of the imprisonment rate during this nearly half a century even led some prominent criminologists to hypothesize a "theory of the stability of punishment."[5] This model suggested that a society develops a certain culture regarding the level of punishment with which it is comfortable, and then, consciously or not, adjusts its policies and practices to meet this desired outcome.

According to the theory, the mechanism for the stability is the use of discretion by actors in the criminal justice system— that is, prosecutors, judges, parole officials, and others make decisions each day concerning what charges to file, what type of sentence to impose, and when to release an offender from prison. Thus, if crime rates or arrest rates increase, these officials may use the discretion available to them to make subtle adjustments in their decision-making regarding sentencing and parole release; conversely, when there is less pressure on the prison system, offenses that may not have previously been perceived as requiring imprisonment may then pass the threshold for incarceration.

While the "stability of punishment" hypothesis may have had some applicability over a period of time, any validity it may have had ceased by the mid-1970s. At that time, the second great "experiment" in the use of incarceration came into being. The first, as we have seen, involved the development of the penitentiary in the eighteenth and nineteenth centuries as a means of controlling deviance through an institutional response. It ultimately failed to achieve many of its objectives, but it nevertheless represented a consciously articulated approach to the problem. The more recent experiment was to see whether a massive and unprecedented use of imprisonment would effectively control crime. It was not an experiment in the usual sense, of course—that is, it was not announced as such, nor would anyone have predicted in 1973 the extreme lengths to which it would evolve over the next quarter century.

The magnitude of the experiment can be measured in many ways. As we see in Figure 2-2, the number of inmates in U.S. state and federal prisons has skyrocketed from 196,000 in 1972 to 1,159,000 by 1997, a 500 percent increase. At the local jail level, the numbers have similarly escalated from 130,000 to 567,000, for a total of more than 1.7 million inmates. Thus, there are now five times as many U.S. citizens locked up as there were twenty-five years ago,[6] for an overall rate of incarceration of 645 inmates per 100,000 population, or about one of every 155 Americans. In addition, more than 100,000 juveniles are locked up in youth facilities across the nation.

We should note here that the figure of one inmate for every 155 U.S. citizens refers to the total U.S. population, including newborns and senior citizens. For those in the peak "prison years" of 20–40, these rates are far higher and, as we shall see later, for African American males, the rates of incarceration can only be described as catastrophic.

To place some perspective on the use of imprisonment in the United States, one can look at other nations for comparison. Figures for 1995, as seen in Table 2-1 and Figure 2-3 show a remarkable story: as we can see, the United States is second only to Russia in its rate of incarceration among the 59 nations in Europe, Asia, and North America for which data are available. (Previous surveys conducted by The Sentencing Project have also documented relatively modest rates of incarceration in South America and some other nations not included here, but comparable data for 1995 were not available.) In contrast to the

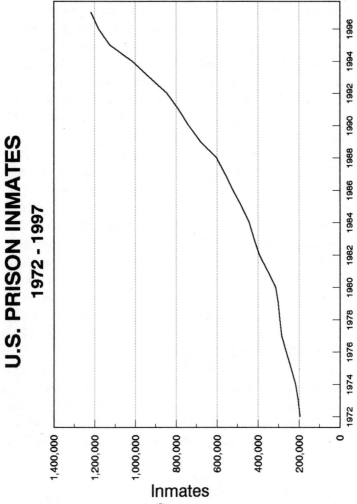

Figure 2-2

U.S. Prison Inmates, 1972–1997

Sources: Bureau of Justice Statistics, *Sourcebook of Criminal Justice Statistics 1996*, Department of Justice, Washington, D.C., 1997, and Bureau of Justice Statistics, "Prison and Jail Inmates at Midyear 1997," 1998

*Note: Data prior to 1977 include only those prisoners held in the custody of state or federal prisons, while remaining years include prisoners under the jurisdiction of state or federal corrections systems, including offenders held in local jails or other institutions.

Table 2-1

International Rates of Incarceration, 1995

Nation	Number of Inmates	Rate of Incarceration per 100,000	Nation	Number of Inmates	Rate of Incarceration per 100,000
Austria	6,761	85	Lithuania	13,228	360
Bangladesh	44,111	37	Luxembourg	469	115
Belarus	52,033	505	Macau	439	107
Belgium	7,401	75	Malaysia	20,324	104
Brunei Darussalam	312	110	Malta	196	55
Bulgaria	9,684	110	Moldova	10,363	275
Cambodia	2,490	26	Netherlands	10,143	65
Canada	33,882	115	New Zealand	4,553	127
China	1,236,534	103	Northern Ireland	1,740	105
Cook Islands	45	225	Norway	2,398	55
Croatia	2,572	55	Philippines	17,843	26
Cyprus	202	30	Poland	65,819	170
Czech Republic	19,508	190	Portugal	12,150	125
Denmark	3,421	65	Romania	45,309	200
England/Wales	51,265	100	Russia	1,017,372	690

Table 2-1 (*continued*)

International Rates of Incarceration, 1995

Nation	Number of Inmates	Rate of Incarceration per 100,000	Nation	Number of Inmates	Rate of Incarceration per 100,000
Estonia	4,034	270	Scotland	5,697	110
Fiji	961	123	Singapore	8,500	287
Finland	3,018	60	Slovakia	7,979	150
France	53,697	95	Slovenia	630	30
Germany	68,396	85	Solomon Islands	150	46
Greece	5,897	55	South Africa	110,120	265
Hong Kong	12,741	207	South Korea	61,019	137
Hungary	12,455	120	Spain	40,157	105
Iceland	113	40	Sweden	5,767	65
India	216,402	24	Switzerland	5,655	80
Ireland	2,032	55	Thailand	106,676	181
Italy	47,323	85	Turkey	49,895	80
Japan	46,622	37	Ukraine	203,988	390
Kiribati	91	130	United States	1,585,401	600
Latvia	9,608	375			

Source: Marc Mauer, *Americans Behind Bars: U.S. and International Use of Incarceration, 1995,* The Sentencing Project, 1997

Figure 2-3

Incarceration Rates for Selected Nations, 1995

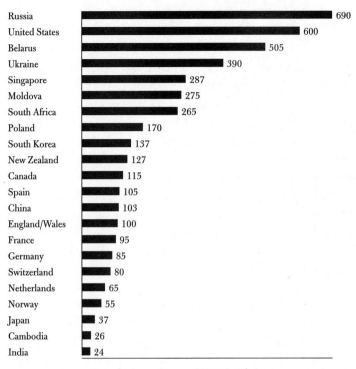

Nation	Rate
Russia	690
United States	600
Belarus	505
Ukraine	390
Singapore	287
Moldova	275
South Africa	265
Poland	170
South Korea	137
New Zealand	127
Canada	115
Spain	105
China	103
England/Wales	100
France	95
Germany	85
Switzerland	80
Netherlands	65
Norway	55
Japan	37
Cambodia	26
India	24

Rate of Incarceration per 100,000 Population

Source: Marc Mauer, *American Behind Bars: U.S. and International Use of Incarceration, 1995,* The Sentencing Project, 1997

industrialized nations to which the United States is most similar, rates of incarceration are about 6–10 times higher in general.

A high rate of incarceration it itself might merely be a reflection of a high crime rate. If so, some would say that this is unfortunate but understandable. A 1994 article by Michael Block, a former member of the U.S. Sentencing Commission, and Steven Twist, head of the NRA's CrimeStrike Division, expressed this sentiment well:

> We are constantly being told that America is now locking-up more
> criminals than at any time in its history, and that these "record" im-
> prisonment rates have had no effect on our crime rates. This "theory"
> now animates most of the policy initiatives on crime from the White
> House, the Justice Department, and the Congress. And yet, nothing
> could be further from the truth.[7]

Block and Twist's political acumen seems rather limited, given
that the "policy initiatives" coming from the White House and
Congress in 1994, the year their article was written, led to a massive federal crime bill authorizing nearly $8 billion in prison
construction funds. More important, though, the authors find
these "record" rates of incarceration of little interest as long as
they "work" to control crime.

Tellingly, though, Block and Twist go on to decry the fact
that federal judges purportedly order prison officials to provide
cable TV and frisbees for inmates, but apparently did not have
sufficient space in their article to make any mention of the demographics of the inmate population. Were they aware of, or
concerned about, the fact that half of the more than one million
people imprisoned at the time were African American? Is this
rate of incarceration the price to be paid for the economic and
social changes that the nation is undergoing in the late twentieth
century? Are there alternative policy approaches that might
"work" to control crime without threatening to "criminalize"
virtually all African American communities? Apparently, in
their zeal to imprison, these questions were of little interest to
the authors.

Such issues are occasionally raised in public discussion,
though often for just a fleeting moment. One occasion was President Clinton's October 1995 address on race relations, which
followed immediately upon the O. J. Simpson criminal trial, the
Million Man March, and The Sentencing Project report documenting that one in three young African American males was
under the control of the criminal justice system.[8] In his talk, the
president asked "every white person here and in America to take
a moment to think how he or she would feel if one in three white

men were in similar circumstances."[9] Unfortunately, as the political history of crime policy will show us, little such reflection is generally conducted either in the White House or on Main Street.

CROSS-NATIONAL CRIME RATE/VICTIMIZATION RATE COMPARISONS

When confronted with data regarding the high comparative rate of incarceration in the United States, one's first reaction is likely to suppose that this can be explained by this country's high crime rate. But is the crime rate uniquely high among nations?

Before we begin an examination of these issues, a word of caution is in order. While one might expect that it would be fairly straightforward to compare crime rates across nations, in fact it is quite difficult. Many nations, even in the industrialized world, maintain different levels and capabilities of record-keeping. Definitions of crime vary as well: a sexual assault in one country may be a rape in another, while it may describe sexual fondling in still a third. Rates of reporting crime vary significantly as well. Again, in regard to sexual assaults, a variety of factors may influence the degree to which victims report these offenses—police receptivity and sensitivity, cultural pressures, or the presence of a feminist movement.

Given these difficulties, comparing official crime statistics across national boundaries becomes quite problematic. One of the more helpful tools for analyzing these issues, though, has been a series of victimization studies conducted in recent years in many industrialized nations. Unlike crime statistics, which measure crimes reported to the police, victimization data are derived from random surveys of households in which citizens are asked if they have been a victim of crime in the preceding time period, whether or not they reported their victimization to the police. Thus, the teenager who has a bike stolen from the garage but doesn't report the theft to the police because he thinks it unlikely to lead to the bike's recovery has been the *victim* of a burglary, but this offense will not show up in the *crime* statistics.

Victimization surveys have been conducted in the United States by the Justice Department since 1972. There have also been three surveys coordinated by the Dutch Ministry of Justice that have compared rates of victimization among nations in the industrialized world for the years 1988, 1991, and 1995. Using a similar methodology for all nations, these surveys have examined rates of victimization for robbery, theft, assault, sexual incidents, vehicle theft, burglary, and other offenses. ("Victimless" crimes such as drug sales are not included in these surveys.)

The surveys find that crime is quite prevalent across most industrialized societies, and that, "with the most obvious exceptions of Japan and Switzerland, all industrialized countries suffer from an appreciable level of property and aggressive crime, particularly in more urbanized areas. Put bluntly, this seems to be the price to be paid for living in an affluent, urbanized and democratic society, regardless of government policy on crime, or the way in which communities try to organize themselves."[10]

In terms of victimization rates in the United States, the results of the eleven nations surveyed in 1996 are rather intriguing, as can be seen in Figure 2-4.

Overall, the U.S. risk of victimization reflects the average for the eleven nations, with 24 percent of the population reporting a victimization in the previous year, comparable to Scotland, France, Canada, and Sweden. Of those victimized, U.S. respondents were somewhat more likely than average to have been victims of burglary and theft of and from cars, while somewhat less likely to have suffered a theft of personal property or vandalization of a car.

A comprehensive analysis of these issues by leading legal scholars has concluded that, for property crimes, U.S. rates are not terribly out of line with comparable nations. Comparing Los Angeles with Sydney, Australia, for example—two cities of roughly the same size—the authors find that Sydney has two-

Figure 2-4

Victimization in Industrialized Nations, 1995

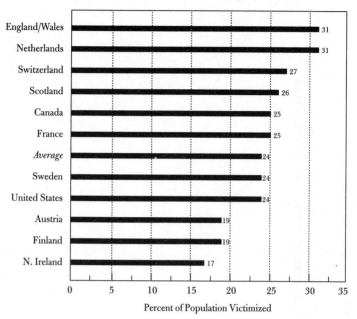

Percent of Population Victimized

Source: Pat Mayhew and Jan J.M. Van Dijk, *Criminal Victimisation in Eleven Industrialized Countries*, Ministry of Justice, The Netherlands, 1997.

thirds the rate of theft as Los Angeles and 10 percent more burglaries. In looking at New York and London, the figures are even more surprising: London's theft rate is 66 percent higher and burglary 57 percent greater.[11]

When we look at rates of violent crime, though, a very different picture emerges. Figure 2-5 shows homicide rates in various nations, as measured per 100,000 persons in the population. In contrast to lesser offenses, the vast majority of homicides are reported to the police in developed nations, so comparisons of these offenses do not involve many of the methodological problems associated with other crimes.

As we can see, the 1996 homicide rate of 7.4 in the United

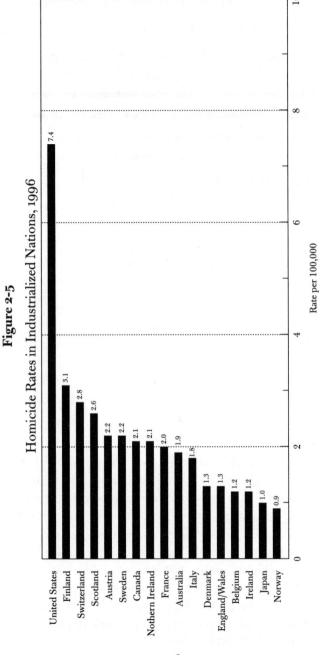

Figure 2-5

Homicide Rates in Industrialized Nations, 1996

Nation	Rate per 100,000
United States	7.4
Finland	3.1
Switzerland	2.8
Scotland	2.6
Austria	2.2
Sweden	2.2
Canada	2.1
Nothern Ireland	2.1
France	2.0
Australia	1.9
Italy	1.8
Denmark	1.3
England/Wales	1.3
Belgium	1.2
Ireland	1.2
Japan	1.0
Norway	0.9

Rate per 100,000

Source: Home Office Research and Statistics Directorate, *Criminal Statistics England and Wales, 1996,* The Stationery Office, England.

28

States is 5–7 times the rate of most industrialized nations. The differential between the United States and other nations is even more remarkable when one considers that its rate of 7.4 per 100,000 was a thirty-year low.

Similar trends among juvenile offenders have been documented by the Department of Justice, which found that juvenile arrest rates for property crimes were similar in the United States and Canada, but that arrest rates for violent crime in the United States were double that of Canada and for murder, six times the Canadian rate.[12]

In dissecting the high murder rate in the United States, we find that a substantial component of the differential is related to homicides committed with firearms. A 1988 comparison of the United States with England/Wales, for example, found that U.S. homicide rates were 5.6 times those of England/Wales. Excluding homicides with firearms, though, yielded a differential of just 2.4 times.[13]

These dramatic disparities should hardly be surprising. As the only major nation with widespread availability of weapons in the home, the potential lethality of the U.S. population is enormous in comparison to other industrialized nations. Also, the propaganda of the National Rifle Association not withstanding, the fact remains that it is far easier to kill someone with a gun than with a knife, fists, or other objects.

The significance of this differential becomes quite apparent when we isolate the impact of policies developed to control guns within a society. This has been illustrated in a comparison of murder rates between the neighboring cities of Seattle in the United States and Vancouver in Canada.[14]

The two cities afford a good basis for comparison because they share many similar characteristics; for example, their population size, racial and ethnic composition, rates of unemployment, and household income were nearly identical during the 1980–86 study period. One area in which they differed substantially was in regard to public policy on firearms: Canada maintained sharp restrictions on the licensing of handguns.

Overall 42 percent of Seattle households possessed handguns, compared to just 12 percent in Vancouver. There is sharp evidence to suggest that the relative availability of guns was the predominant factor contributing to crime differentials. Burglary rates in the two cities were nearly identical, but the rate of aggravated assault was higher in Seattle. Disaggregating these data, though, showed that the rate of assaults with knives, clubs, and fists was virtually the same in the two cities, but that the firearm assault rate in Seattle was eight times higher than in Vancouver.

An examination of homicide rates confirmed the significance of handgun availability as a major contributing factor to violent crime. Over a seven-year period, the number of homicides in Seattle (388) was considerably higher than in Vancouver (204). But the rate of homicides committed with knives and other weapons excluding firearms was virtually the same. Thus, almost the entire difference in homicide rates between the two cities was due to the more widespread availability of firearms in Seattle.

CRIME RATES AND THE RISE IN INCARCERATION IN THE UNITED STATES

The United States, then, has a higher rate of violent crime, but not necessarily of property crime, than comparable nations. To what extent does the high rate of violent crime explain the dramatic increase in the use of prison since the 1970s or the relative distinctions with other nations?

Clearly, some of the rise in imprisonment in the 1970s was due to increasing rates of violence. Crime rates and violent crime rose during the 1960s for a host of reasons. The changing demographics of that period—the coming of age of the "baby boom" population in particular—provided a larger group of young males in the traditional high-crime-rate years. Increasing urbanization also may have contributed to more crime, in part due to the loosening of social bonds that are often more prevalent in smaller communities.

The degree to which crime rates rose in the 1960s is not easy to determine. Unfortunately, FBI data from that period are fairly unreliable, at least by current standards. Many police departments either did not participate in the annual Uniform Crime Reports surveys or provided incomplete data, and so the actual level of crime in the 1960s is very much understated. These partial data have since been used by a number of pro-incarceration advocates to suggest that the rise in crime after the 1960s was more substantial than was actually the case.

For example, the American Legislative Exchange Council (ALEC), a self-described association of state legislators "advancing policies which expand free markets, promote economic growth, limit government and preserve individual liberties," contends that crime rates overall rose by 215 percent from 1960 to 1980, and violent crime by 271 percent during the period;[15] but if the figure for 1960 was an undercount, as it surely was, then the overall rate of increase for this period must be considerably less.

Looking at murder rates provides us with closer estimates of changes in crime, since the reporting rate for murder has always been higher than for other offenses. Here, ALEC reports a 100 percent increase from 1960 to 1980, but fails to draw the obvious conclusion regarding the significance of this figure for understanding crime rate trends: if murder rates "only" rose by 100 percent, it is highly unlikely that rates of robbery rose by 318 percent and rape by 283 percent, as claimed by ALEC in their uncritical look at the FBI data. Rather, it is far more likely that *reporting* of these offenses both by victims and police agencies increased substantially, thereby accounting for a significant portion of the reported increase.

But even if one accounts for underreporting, the bulk of the increase in violent crime occurred between 1960 and 1974. Again, looking at murder rates as the most reliable indicator of trends, we find that the number of murders rose from 9,110 in 1960 to 20,710 by 1974, or a rate increase of 5.0 to 9.8 per

100,000. Then, for a period of twenty years, murder rates fluctuated within a range of 8.5–10 per 100,000.

If violent crime "only" doubled in the 1960s and 1970s, this undoubtedly contributed to the rise of the prison population that began in 1973. But this rise was hardly the only reason; political considerations came to have an increasingly significant influence.

NONVIOLENT OFFENSES AND THE CONTINUING RISE IN IMPRISONMENT

By the beginning of the 1980s, the crime policies of the "get tough" movement were well under way. An analysis of the growth in the use of prison from that time until the present undermines the contention that the continuing race to incarcerate in the United States is a result of higher rates of violent crime.

There are two profitable approaches to measuring the use of imprisonment during this period. The first regards the number of people receiving a prison *sentence* during this time period. As we can see in Table 2-2, there were 154,361 more offenders sentenced to prison in 1995 than 1985, for an increase of 84 percent. The vast majority of this increase, though (77 percent) consisted of nonviolent drug and property offenders; drug offenders alone accounted for over half the increase. Less than one in four (23 percent) of the increase in the number of sentenced felony offenders had been convicted of a violent offense.

This trend suggests that judges are sentencing more offenders to prison for all offenses. In many cases, this has been a result of legislatively enacted mandatory sentencing policies that require a prison sentence for certain offenses, regardless of mitigating factors. This trend has been particularly significant for drug offenses, where the risk of receiving a prison sentence following an arrest rose by fully 447 percent between 1980 and 1992.[16]

The second approach is to examine the increase in the number of people *in* prison, as opposed to those sentenced to

Table 2-2

Increase in New Sentences to State Prison by Crime Type, 1985–95

Offense	Prison Sentences 1985	Prison Sentences 1995	Increase 1985–95	% Increase	% of Total Increase
Total	183,131	337,492	154,361	84%	100%
Violent	64,300	99,400	35,100	55%	23%
Property	77,600	97,600	20,000	26%	13%
Drug	24,200	104,400	80,200	331%	52%
Public order, other	17,100	36,100	19,000	111%	12%

Note: Due to rounding, columns do not add up to 100%. Data calculated from Bureau of Justice Statistics reports.

prison. Since nonviolent offenders generally receive shorter sentences than violent offenders, the prison population tends to reflect more of the longer-term inmates and, therefore, a higher proportion of violent offenders than do those who receive a prison sentence.

As we can see in Table 2-3, two trends of interest emerge here. First, in absolute terms, there was a significant increase in the number of violent offenders who were imprisoned during this time, rising from 246,200 in 1985 to 457,600 by 1995. On a proportional basis, though, the increase in incarcerated drug offenders is more dramatic, with a 478 percent rise during this period.

If we look further at the overall use of prison space, we find that new prison cells are increasingly being used for drug and other nonviolent offenders. Thus, about three of every five (61 percent) new inmates added to the system in this decade were incarcerated for a nonviolent drug or property offense. The impact of drug policies on the federal prison system is even more dramatic, with drug offenses alone accounting for three fourths (74 pecent) of the rise in the inmate population between 1985 and 1995, as seen in Table 2-4.

Looking at the overall factors leading to the rise in incarceration, research has demonstrated that changes in criminal justice policy, rather than changes in crime rates, have been the most significant contributors leading to the rise in state prison populations. A regression analysis of the rise in the number of inmates from 1980 to 1996 concluded that one half (51.4 percent) of the increase was explained by a greater likelihood of a prison sentence upon arrest, one third (36.6 percent) by an increase in time served in prison, and just one ninth (11.5 percent) by higher offense rates.[17]

Incarcerating ever-increasing numbers of nonviolent property and drug offenders is hardly the only option available to policymakers, nor is it necessarily the most cost-effective. A study of the California prison population funded by the California legislature concluded that as many as a quarter of incoming

Table 2-3

State Prison Inmates by Offense, 1985–95

Offense	Inmates 1985	Inmates 1995	Increase	% Increase	% of Total Increase
Total	451,812	989,007	537,195	119%	100%
Violent	246,200	457,600	211,400	86%	39%
Property	140,100	237,400	97,300	69%	18%
Drug	38,900	224,900	186,000	478%	35%
Public order, other	26,200	69,100	42,900	164%	8%

Note: Due to rounding, columns do not add up to 100%. Data calculated from Bureau of Justice Statistics reports.

Table 2-4

Federal Prison Inmates by Offense, 1985–95

Offense	1985	1995	Increase	% Increase	% of Total Increase
Total	31,364	88,101	56,737	181%	100%
Violent	7,768	11,321	3,553	46%	6%
Property	5,289	7,524	2,235	42%	4%
Drug	9,482	51,737	42,255	446%	74%
Public order, other	8,825	17,519	8,694	99%	15%

Note: Due to rounding, columns do not add up to 100%. Data calculated from Bureau of Justice Statistics reports.

inmates to the prison system would be appropriate candidates for diversion to community-based programs. This group would include offenders sentenced to prison for technical violations of parole, minor drug use, or nonviolent property offenses. The study estimated that diverting such offenders would save 17–20 percent of the corrections operating budget for new prison admissions.[18] Other commentators have suggested that even higher rates of diversion are possible.

INTERNATIONAL COMPARISONS

As we have seen, the United States has a higher violent crime rate than other nations, particularly for violence committed with firearms, but relatively comparable rates of crime for other offenses. A comprehensive review of the relatively modest amount of research looking at the United States in comparison to other nations in this regard confirms that both higher rates of violent offenses as well as harsher criminal justice policies for some offenses distinguish the United States from other industrialized nations.[19]

The study of the prevalence of incarceration in the United States, Canada, England/Wales, and the former West Germany found that, for violent offenses, with the exception of West Germany, these nations had comparable rates of incarceration given the numbers of arrests for these crimes. Substantial differences emerge, though, with regard to punishment for property crimes. Burglars in the United States, for example, served an average of 16.2 months in prison, compared to 5.3 months in Canada and 6.8 months in England, and U.S. larceny offenders served about 3–6 times as long as those in Canada. While comparative data for drug offenses are more limited, at least one study that compared the United States with England/Wales found that U.S. drug offenders were considerably more likely to be sentenced to prison and for a longer period of time.[20]

The author concludes that "in the case of property crime, it is clear that the United States incarcerates more and for longer periods of time than other similar nations. The same appears to be true for drug offenses." He further suggests that reasonably large reductions in the prison population could be achieved by reducing the use of incarceration and length of crime served for property crime (and possibly drug offenses) to the level of nations like England or Canada.[21]

How to achieve those kinds of prison population reductions is a complex issue that involves an understanding of both criminal justice policies and societal attitudes. Criminologists Warren Young and Mark Brown have examined variations in incarceration among a number of nations in Europe as well as New Zealand and Australia.[22] Their statistical analysis concludes that "only a small measure of the differences in prison populations between one jurisdiction and another or the changes in prison populations within particular jurisdictions seem to be related to crime rates. Moreover, to the extent that there is a relationship, we cannot be certain that it is a causal one; both official crime rates and prison rates may be affected by the level of punitiveness in a society—that is, attitudes toward crime and punishment may influence known criminality as well as sentencing practice."[23]

Young and Brown identify two key factors that determine the size of a nation's prison population: the rate at which offenders are *admitted* to prison and the length of time that offenders *serve* in prison. In other words, it is possible that Nation A sentences many offenders to prison but for a relatively short time, whereas Nation B sentences fewer offenders to prison but for relatively longer periods. Both countries might have similar rates of incarceration, but would attain them through very different means.

Young and Brown's statistical analysis concludes that sentence length is a more critical variable than prison admissions in determining the relative size of prison populations. In looking at the Netherlands and Sweden, for example, both of which have low rates of incarceration, they find that the rate of sentencing to prison is comparable to other nations, but that shorter average sentences account for the difference in incarceration rates.

This statistical presentation makes intuitive sense as well. If a nation or a jurisdiction hopes to lower its rate of incarceration through a reduction in the *number* of offenders sentenced to prison, this policy would be most likely to target offenders who receive the shortest prison sentences, since presumably they represent less of a public safety threat than others in the inmate population. But while inmates with short sentences may comprise a fair proportion of admissions to prison, they comprise a much smaller share of the total prison population, which is driven more by those offenders serving long terms. Therefore, a greater impact on overall prison populations is more likely to be achieved through changes in the length of time served in prison.

A society's level of incarceration may be related to its political or economic structure as well. Research by Leslie Wilkins and Ken Pease suggests that a "society's penal climate or its relative punitiveness is linked to its relative egalitarianism: the greater a society's tolerance of inequality, the more extreme the scale of punishment utilized."[24] Thus, sentencing severity is a type of negative reward for those at one end of the spectrum, compared to the positive rewards of income and status. A society such as the United States, which contains a greater disparity of wealth than other industrialized nations, will therefore be more likely to display harsher cultural attitudes toward sentencing policy than will a nation with a broader social welfare outlook and system.

The practical impact of this proposition can be seen in some European nations. In the Scandinavian countries, for example, it is not unusual to participate in policy discussions regarding the "appropriate" level of incarceration in a society, with scant regard for crime rates. For example, beginning in the mid-1970s, officials in Finland introduced changes in criminal justice policy designed to lower the national rate of incarceration out of concern that their use of imprisonment was abnormally high by Scandinavian standards. By U.S. standards, this type of approach is a bit jarring, since public dialogue on imprisonment all but assumes that the only critical variable is the level of crime. Clearly, though, this assumption is far from universal. While the analysis of comparative incarceration rates is subject to debate, what seems clear is that the issue is far more complex than conventional political or public discourse often suggests. The degree to which a society engages in prison-building, far from illustrating a direct correlation between crime and incarceration, is subject to a host of decisions made within and outside the criminal justice system.

NOTES

1. David J. Rothman, *The Discovery of the Asylum: Social Order and Disorder in the New Republic* (Boston: Little, Brown, 1971), p. 295 (emphasis added).
2. National Advisory Commission on Criminal Justice Standards and Goals, *Task Force Report on Corrections* (Washington, D.C.: Government Printing Office, 1973), p. 358.
3. Ibid., p. 597.
4. Margaret Werner Cahalan, *Historical Corrections Statistics in the United States, 1850–1984* (Washington, D.C.: Bureau of Justice Statistics, December 1986), pp. 35, 77.
5. Alfred Blumstein and Jacqueline Cohen, "A Theory of the Stability of Punishment," *Journal of Criminal Law and Criminology* 64 (1973), pp. 198–207.
6. Note that while the number of inmates in prison is six times that of twenty-five years ago, as previously reported, the number of inmates in prison *or* jail is five times the 1972 figure.
7. Michael K. Block and Steven J. Twist, "Lessons from the Eighties: Incarceration Works," *Commonsense* 1 (Spring 1994), p. 76.
8. Marc Mauer and Tracy Huling, *Young Black Americans and the Criminal Justice System: Five Years Later* (Washington, D.C.: The Sentencing Project, 1995), p. 1.
9. William J. Clinton, text of address, *Washington Post*, October 17, 1995.
10. Jan J.M. van Dijk and Patricia Mayhew, *Criminal Victimisation in the Industrialized World* (Netherlands: Ministry of Justice, November 1992), p. 55.
11. Franklin E. Zimring and Gordon Hawkins, *Crime Is Not the Problem: Lethal Violence in America* (Oxford, Eng.: Oxford University Press, 1997), pp. 4–6.
12. Melissa Sickmund, Howard N. Snyder, and Eileen Poe-Yamagata, *Juvenile Offenders and Victims: 1997 Update on Violence* (Washington, D.C.: Office of Juvenile Justice and Delinquency Prevention, June 1997), p. 36.
13. James Lynch, "Crime in International Perspective," in James Q. Wilson and Joan Petersilia, eds., *Crime* (San Francisco: Institute for Contemporary Studies, 1995), pp. 22–23.
14. Carl T. Bogus, "The Strong Case for Gun Control," *American Prospect* (Summer 1992), pp. 19–28.
15. American Legislative Exchange Council, *Report Card on Crime and Punishment*

(Washington, D.C.: American Legislative Exchange Council, October 1994), p. 9.

16. Allen J. Beck and Darrell K. Gilliard, *Prisoners in 1994* (Washington, D.C.: Bureau of Justice Statistics, 1995), p. 13.

17. Alfred Blumstein and Allen J. Beck, "Factors Contributing to the Growth in U.S. Prison Populations," in Michael Tonry and Joan Petersilia, eds., *Crime and Justice: A Review of Research*, vol. 23 (Chicago: University of Chicago Press, forthcoming 1999).

18. Joan Petersilia, "Diverting Nonviolent Prisoners to Intermediate Sanctions: The Impact on California Prison Admissions and Corrections Costs," *Corrections Management Quarterly* 1.1 (1997), p. 8.

19. Lynch, "Crime in an International Perspective," pp. 11–38.

20. Ibid., p. 36.

21. Ibid., p. 37.

22. Warren Young and Mark Brown, "Cross-national Comparisons of Imprisonment," in Michael Tonry, ed., *Crime and Justice: A Review of Research*, vol. 17 (Chicago: University of Chicago Press, 1993), pp. 1–49.

23. Ibid., p. 33.

24. Ibid., p. 41.

3—The Development of the "Tough on Crime" Movement

The Rise and Decline of Rehabilitation

W hile the race to incarcerate formally began with the rise of the prison population in 1973, its roots can be traced to political currents and socio-economic changes of the previous decade. Within the realm of crime policy, foremost among these changes was a critique of rehabilitation which involved an unusual coalescence between forces on the left and the right.

While the prison as an institution has changed surprisingly little over two centuries, its functions in society, as perceived by both practitioners and the public, have undergone a series of philosophical shifts. The notion of deterrence was uppermost in the minds of the founders of the prison models which began just after the colonial period; these evolved into a system that took on the goal of rehabilitation in the Jacksonian period—and that goal has been a guiding principle of the system throughout much of the twentieth century. The approach assumes—based on sociological, psychological, or moral beliefs—that an offender is someone who has erred but is capable of change, and that the period of incarceration can be viewed as a time to effect interventions that may bring about more law-abiding behavior.

The first decades after World War II represented a modern peak in the influence of the rehabilitative ideal on the corrections system. The country was emerging from a deadly but victorious conflict; the "baby boom" that followed in its wake brought on an era of hopefulness and optimism about the future. With the United States escaping from the war relatively unscathed on the home front, visions of an "American Century" became enticing to many business and political leaders.

This emerging economic might and sense of rebirth influenced public attitudes on social policy in a variety of ways. An expanding economic pie potentially meant greater goods and services, and allowed for more compassionate and generous public policy responses to social problems. In regard to crime and justice, this laid the groundwork for growing support for a broader acceptance of the goal of rehabilitation. We can see this perhaps most clearly in public attitudes on the death penalty. While the death penalty has been employed since the colonial period, it reached its peak of use in modern times during the Depression, with as many as 199 persons being executed annually by 1935. By the 1950s, though, the pace of executions had slowed to less than half that rate, and by 1963, there were just 23 executions.[1]

This decline does not appear to have reflected any dramatic drop in the number of murders; rather, it seems to reflect a growing public unease with the use of the ultimate punishment. Survey data show declining support for use of the death penalty in the postwar era, reaching a low of 42 percent support in 1966.[2] A newly energized abolitionist movement gained strength as well, motivated in part by such celebrated cases as those of Julius and Ethel Rosenberg and Caryl Chesman in California.

As public opposition mounted, legal challenges to executions began to develop as well, so that by the late 1960s, executions all but ceased as it became clear that only a Supreme Court decision would resolve the issue. Thus, in 1972, in *Furman v. Georgia*, the court ruled that the Georgia death penalty statute was cruel and unusual in its application—and, because the same infirmities existed in the statutes of other states, they were all in effect declared unconstitutional. The decision removed all inmates from Death Row and halted death sentences nationally, but only until the court ruled in 1976 that statutes which defined more specifically the circumstances under which death could be imposed were permissible.

The postwar move toward abolition of capital punishment was accompanied by support for rehabilitation within prison as well. As late as 1968, a Harris poll showed that 48 percent of the public thought that the primary purpose of prison *was* rehabilitation and that 72 percent believed the emphasis *should be* on rehabilitation.[3]

During the 1960s, though, this support for rehabilitation was challenged from two very distinct directions. From the left came a broad critique of the concept of rehabilitation in an inherently coercive institution such as a prison. Numerous liberal critics wondered whether the nature of personal transformation required a voluntary desire for change, and they questioned whether it could be accomplished under conditions of forced confinement. This critique, of course, applied not only to prisons but to other institutions as well, particularly mental hospitals.

In the influential book *Struggle for Justice*, the Working Party of the American Friends Service Committee gave voice to this concern:

> Mixing treatment with coercion in the penal system not only lengthens sentences and increases the suffering and the sense of injustice, it also vitiates the treatment programs that are its justification. . . . Beyond the special problems of effecting "treatment" in prisons, is it possible to coerce people into "treatment" in any setting? Is the necessary therapeutic relationship between the helper and the helped possible if the person to be helped is forced into the relationship?[4]

This challenge was bolstered on the left by the growing belief that prisoners represented an oppressed class whose crimes resulted from their second-class status in society. Given the substantial numbers of black and Hispanic inmates in the prison system, many of whom gave explicit voice to a political consciousness that challenged the notion of an unbiased justice system, supporters on the outside began to draw connections between the burgeoning civil rights movement and the demands for a fairer system of justice.

As the civil rights and antiwar movements blossomed, activists in these causes gained a heightened understanding of the prison system—in part because protestors began to be arrested in large numbers. Some spent a night in jail, others months or even years in prison; however, all who went through the experience at least had a modest sense of the experience of being locked up.

Growing numbers of sociologists and people on the left also came to see crime as essentially learned behavior that was a rational, if illegal, response to a set of social conditions. Efforts to reduce crime, they argued, should focus on alleviating the social, economic, and political marginality of the poor. In policy and programmatic terms, this led to such efforts as the Model Cities program and the welfare rights movement of the 1960s.

For many, then, prisons and the entire criminal justice apparatus came to be perceived as unjust institutions that served to reinforce the status quo. Given this perspective, there was little reason to support rehabilitation, even if it were possible, since its accomplishments would only reinforce the existing social structure.

This critique of the prison system was most pointed in its attack on the structure of sentencing. For nearly one hundred years prior, the indeterminate sentencing system had prevailed in almost all state systems. Under this structure, a judge would impose both a minimum and maximum term of imprisonment on a convicted offender. The maximum term was established by the legislature for the particular offense and the minimum sentence set the earliest date at which the inmate could be considered for parole release.

The rationale for the indeterminate sentence was tied to the prospect of rehabilitation in the prison setting. It was believed that if an inmate was to be encouraged to take advantage of programming in prison (however meager that might be at times), a reward system should be in place. There could be no better reward than release from prison. So, theoretically at least, inmates would have incentives to engage in educational or vocational programming and to conduct themselves responsibly in order to earn their release as quickly as possible. The system also had the value of providing wardens and guards with a powerful tool to enforce prison discipline. With a decision by a parole board contingent in part on an inmate's behavior, prison officials wielded a very tempting "carrot" to accompany the "stick" of prison disciplinary measures.

Within the framework of the indeterminate sentence, though, lay its potential for abuse and injustice. The open-ended nature of the sentence meant that prison officials and boards of parole maintained broad discretion in deciding how long any given imprisonment would last. While the goal of rehabilitation may have served as the rationale for such a policy, in practice broad variations in decision-making resulting in bias on the basis of race, gender, and other factors were far too common.

It was this potential for the arbitrary use of authority in race- and class-biased ways that bolstered the left critique of sentencing. The celebrated case of George Jackson, the "Soledad Brother" in California, illustrated this well. Jackson, an articulate and radical leader of the prison movement of the late 1960s, had been convicted of stealing seventy dollars in a gas station holdup at the age of 18; he received a sentence of 1–70 years. In 1969, he and two other African American inmates were charged with the beating death of a prison guard, charges that were later dismissed after a national support campaign.

By the late 1960s, Jackson's supporters both inside prison and on the outside despaired of his ever earning his release, viewing his challenge to authority and to the prison system as a virtual guarantee of a life sentence. Indeed, with Ronald Reagan serving as governor of California at the time, and with great official hostility to the burgeoning black political movement, it seemed quite unlikely that Jackson would earn his release in the near future. In a fiery conclusion to his national saga, Jackson was shot and killed by prison guards in San Quentin in 1971, while allegedly trying to escape with a gun believed to be smuggled into prison by his attorney. A few months later, the Attica prison rebellion in New York resulted in the deaths of 43 inmates and guards by state troopers overtaking the prison.

Coinciding with the left–liberal challenge to sentencing was an attack from the political right. Frustrated by rising crime rates in the 1960s, the "pro-defendant" decisions of the Warren Supreme Court, and growing liberal opposition to the Vietnam War and other government policies, conservatives took on the issue of crime as the centerpiece of a political program. Barry Goldwater's presidential campaign in 1964, followed by Richard Nixon's campaign in 1968, heralded the theme of "law and order" for the first time in a national political context. While the "order" they were calling for was a broad response to urban unrest and antiwar protest, it also projected a not very subtle message to whites concerned with the supposed rise in black criminal behavior.

The conservatives' principal approach was to challenge the indeterminate sentencing system. First, they asserted that the system permitted the early release of offenders who deserved a lengthier prison term. Criminals "are going free in droves," was the message of *The Lawbreakers*, promising that crime could be cut in half if convicted offenders were made to serve out their full sentences.[5] Conservatives also objected to the rehabilitative underpinnings of the system both because they lacked confidence in the feasibility of rehabilitation and because a definite and punitive sentence as a response to crime seemed to them to be more appropriate and more feasible. For example, James Q. Wilson, a Harvard professor whose *Thinking About Crime* was very influential at the time, expressed skepticism about evidence which suggested that rehabilitative programs had any value; instead, he argued that the function of the corrections system should be "to isolate and to punish."[6] This would then provide "recognition that a society at a minimum must be able to protect itself from dangerous offenders and to impose some costs (other than the stigma and inconvenience of an arrest and court appearance) on criminal acts; it is also a frank admission that society really does not know how to do much else."[7]

The positions of both liberals and conservatives were bolstered by an influential article by Robert Martinson that appeared in the journal *The Public Interest* in 1974.[8] Martinson's basic question—what works?—was drawn from a larger study he had conducted with two colleagues. In short, their review of 231 evaluations of juvenile and adult corrections programs suggested that "nothing works." Martinson contended that "with few and isolated exceptions, the rehabilitative efforts that have been reported so far have had no appreciable effect on rehabilitation."[9]

Martinson's conclusions were challenged by many in the field for painting too sweeping a picture of failure and not paying sufficient attention to signs of success in specific instances. Martinson himself later reconsidered his broad conclusions in a journal article that received far less attention than the original; he and other researchers came to believe that some programs work for some offenders some of the time. The challenge for policymakers and practitioners, then, was to isolate the factors that encouraged success and to refine further the conditions under which rehabilitative projects would meet the needs of a range of offenders.

But these refinements came too late. Martinson's original conclusion was immediately hailed by the left as confirming that rehabilitation indeed was impossible in a coercive setting and by the right as proof that rehabilitation was not even worth trying. It thus lent support to a growing belief from both directions that a more fixed and determinate sentencing structure, one that decreased emphasis on rehabilitation, would be an improvement over the prevailing system. The only substantial disagreement among the contending parties concerned the length of prison terms to be imposed.

Liberals such as those convened for the American Friends Service Committee's *Struggle for Justice* called for short, fixed prison sentences. In addition, "There is to be no discretion in setting sentences, no indeterminate sentences, and unsupervised street release is to replace parole."[10] The rationale for this was both to reduce the harm that might be caused by imprisonment and to reduce or eliminate the abuse inherent in the indeterminate sentencing system. Under this type of proposal, an inmate would know exactly how long he or she would be locked up and this time frame, with only modest reductions for "good time," would be unaltered. Once such a system were in place, the liberals had no objection to prisoners partaking of any educational or vocational programs that might be offered in prison, since these would then be engaged in on a voluntary basis, and not tied to a release date.

Meanwhile, conservatives too argued for fixed terms, but generally favored lengthier sentences. Since rehabilitation had now been discredited, the prison system could get on with its objective of incapacitating criminals. After all, an offender who was locked up was not able to commit crimes on the streets. The apparent simplicity of this model led to its successful adoption in public and political rhetoric; these themes would be echoed for the succeeding twenty years.

Whether the liberal support for determinate sentencing was a wise idea is quite debatable, both from a theoretical and a practical perspective. In assessing this movement several years after its inception, the late criminologist Donald Cressey stated:

> In democracies, nondiscretionary sentencing systems always give power to the legislative branch of government, as compared to the judicial and executive branches. The power is the same as that seized by dictators who tolerate no breaches of their orders. . . . Currently, legislators are using the justice model of sentencing to restrict the freedom of courthouse personnel (and other criminal justice workers as well) to be wise, compassionate, innovative, judicious, and fair. Judges are being directed to impose fixed amounts of pain on criminals in a machine-like manner.[11]

Nevertheless, the philosophical lines were drawn regarding the direction of sentencing policy in the United States. Had these been just academic debates among partisans in the field, perhaps they would not have had much meaning. However, changes in the political climate would rapidly create opportunities for implementing many of the most punitive proposals within just a few years.

3—The "Tough on Crime" Movement Triumphs

Although the debate on sentencing policy had been conducted in both the academic world and within the realm of the criminal justice system, its roots extended well into the social and political changes that had begun to emerge with great force in the 1960s. Foremost among these was the issue of race. Issues of race and class have always been intertwined with the development and use of the U.S. prison system, but the changes that emerged in the 1960s marked a new era in the national approach to crime policy and its attendant impact on African Americans in particular.

Among the many legacies to U.S. society of the 1960s was an increase in rates of crime and violence. As noted earlier, we don't really know to what extent crime rates actually increased; one of the ironies of the period is that the growing politicization of crime itself contributed to higher reporting rates. The primary way in which this came about was through the creation of the Law Enforcement Assistance Administration (LEAA) as part of the Safe Streets Act passed by Congress in 1967.

LEAA provided for a new and dramatically enlarged federal role in crime-fighting, primarily by making funding available to state and local governments. In the first several years of its existence, LEAA grants skyrocketed from $300 million in 1968 to $1.25 billion in 1974.[12] Much of the early funding was provided for local police departments to purchase hardware and to upgrade technology. The new technology, along with training from federal officials, led to considerably higher rates of crime reporting from police agencies to the FBI for inclusion in its annual crime reports.

While crime rates did increase in the 1960s many conservatives portrayed this as a unique historical development and contrasted it with the image of a more idyllic America where "crime in the streets" was relatively unknown. This ignored, of course, the entire history of the "Wild West," street crime battles among the various waves of immigrant groups, and Depression-era gangster violence. By the 1980s, we would see Ronald Reagan's "Morning in America" campaign themes painting a warm picture of small-town (white) America where people worked hard, got along, had a strong sense of family, and, presumably, were unplagued by crime.

The conservative portrait lacked any historical perspective, but it did not fail to capitalize on the real and sobering increase in crime. In retrospect, there should have been many indications that such a rise was likely in the 1960s. The coming of age of the "baby boom" generation brought with it an unprecedented number of young males in the high crime years of 15–24. While most of them never committed any serious offense, their sheer numbers alone were likely to contribute to at least a partial surge in crime.

The 1960s also brought the inception of the first of what were to be three drug epidemics over a thirty-year period. As heroin swept through many urban areas in the 1960s, so would cocaine in the late 1970s, and then crack cocaine in the 1980s. Each episode would lead to a series of legislative and policy changes focused on punitive responses to the prevailing drug problem—changes that would significantly contribute to a harshening of criminal justice policy during these decades.

A key factor behind the rise in crime rates was the rapid urbanization of the population. For a complex set of reasons, urbanization is generally equated with higher rates of crime. The relative stresses and strains of urban life, the increased significance of neighborhood and peer group influences at the expense of the immediate family, the breakdown of cultural and organizational structures brought from the "old world," and perhaps the lure of more consumer goods—all these things generally result in higher than average crime rates in urban areas.

Much of the demographic shift and increasing urbanization

was attributable to movements of large segments of the black population and to a somewhat lesser extent, whites and Hispanics. The postwar years were a time of mass migration, most notably from the rural black South and the hills of white Appalachia to the growing industrial economies of midwestern and northern cities. As the auto and steel industries mushroomed in Detroit, Akron, Baltimore, and other areas, relatively well-paid jobs for working class men (and sometimes women) fueled these demographic shifts. Blacks had been disproportionately affected by the shift to mechanized agriculture in the South, which was contemporaneous with the increased demand for labor in the growing northern economies. The movement of five million black people from the South to the North between 1940 and 1970 reduced the proportion of African Americans who lived in the South from three fourths to just half in this thirty-year period.[13]

The postwar period also witnessed the burgeoning of the civil rights movement—most prominent in the South, it spread rapidly to all parts of the country. As the movement grew, it led to Black Power and other offshoots; however, a resistant political culture often attempted to thwart its efforts. By the mid-1960s, the growing sense of injustice, the tragic assassinations of the era, and incidents of police brutality resulted in the "hot summer" of 1967 and the urban rebellions following the murder of Martin Luther King.

White reaction to such rebellions often failed to distinguish them from the growing civil rights and antiwar protests, on the one hand, and traditional crimes of an economic or violent nature, on the other. Instead, all of these phenomena were subsumed under the heading of "crime in the streets." This fuzzy logic was in large measure endorsed, at least implicitly, both by supporters and by opponents of the civil rights movement. Some leftists considered crime and urban unrest a response by an oppressed class to an unjust system; this kind of analysis tended to ignore the fact that many of the victims of these crimes were members of the oppressed class themselves. Opponents of the growing social movements of the 1960s were equally careless about the distinction between "ordinary" crimes and politically inspired urban unrest. Thus, George Wallace argued that "the same Supreme Court that ordered integration and encouraged civil rights legislation" was now "bending over backwards to help criminals."[14] Then in 1968, Richard Nixon's famous campaign call for "law and order" spoke to these fears, hostilities, and racist underpinnings. By this point, the issue had been reframed in these terms to such a degree that a 1969 poll reported that 81 percent of the public believed that law and order had broken down, with a majority blaming "Negroes who start riots" and "communists."[15]

Thus were the seeds sown for a movement that would ultimately get so "tough" on crime that it would result in world record rates of incarceration. In a nation with a centuries-long history of racial conflict and oppression, it was probably not surprising that the newly inspired approach to social problems emphasized a stepped-up use of the criminal justice apparatus at the expense of other choices. It would be a mistake to dismiss the entire preoccupation with crime as some type of racist plot unrelated to any real concerns, but the *method of choice* for responding to those concerns undoubtedly reflected racial biases and perceptions. Those most in danger of being victimized, for example, were not necessarily the most punitive in their attitudes, and vice versa. Much of this correlates with race. One scholar concludes that, "despite the fact that rates of criminal victimization are much higher among blacks, for example, it is whites who have historically been more supportive of punitive anticrime measures. . . . White punitiveness in particular seems to be largely inexplicable in terms of one's 'risk profile.' "[16]

Other, more legitimate, factors contributed to the "get tough" movement, including the growing feminist movement of the 1960s and 1970s. Whether women were now more vulnerable than in previous generations or just less willing to suffer victimization in silence, they increasingly gave voice to a demand for protection and safety, extending their demands to ensure their own freedom to walk the streets in safety and punish perpetrators of sexual violence. This movement encompassed a variety of ideological orientations; some emphasized the need for cultural and behavioral change, while others stressed the need for a stepped-up punitive response. Additional support for harsher policies was available from middle-aged and elderly people as well, people who wielded political power in society and who could recall a time in life when they felt much safer.

The rise in crime of the 1960s, along with the increased fear that accompanied it, ironically began during relatively prosperous economic times and in an era of rising expectations. These conditions were not to last long, though. By 1973, American business met a stumbling block with the imposition of the Arab oil embargo. The accelerating decline of the U.S. auto and steel industries quickly followed, later accompanied by the now-commonplace "downsizing" of industries and employees. While the American economy of the late 1990s is relatively robust (if not equitably distributed), it is nevertheless marked by a high degree of volatility and uncertainty, concern about budget deficits, and reduced expectations among much of the population.

These changes affected crime and criminal justice policy in a number of ways. Tighter budgets at all levels of government created a situation where the economic pie had ceased to expand and was now being carved up into ever-smaller pieces. It proved far easier to advocate increased government spending of the "Great Society" type in the 1960s when the economy was growing, than during periods of recession and retrenchment. The low-income communities from which most prisoners came were hardly politically influential in head-to-head competition with the Pentagon or even with middle-class taxpayers seeking more funds for suburban schools.

Sociologist Dario Melossi offers a theory of the means by which punitive crime policies emerge in times of economic stress. Using a class-based analysis of conflict, he contends that, as more working families find themselves in a state of economic uncertainty, power elites perceive this situation as an impending crisis. Potential labor insubordination is then interpreted as a "general moral malaise of society," which leads to a cultural redefinition of a variety of social conditions, including a harshening of punishment policies.[17]

By the 1980s, the impact of the Reagan budget cuts and stepped-up military spending reduced the fiscal capacity for a broad-based activist government response to social problems. This in turn helped to lay the groundwork for an ideological and policy sea change that emphasized "social defense" through the military and crime control apparatus at the expense of social investments in communities. "Getting tough" on crime was now the order of the day.

NOTES

1. Bureau of Justice Statistics, *Correctional Populations in the United States, 1994* (Washington, D.C.: Bureau of Justice Statistics, June 1996), p. 172.
2. "Gallup Poll Monthly," as summarized in *Sourcebook of Criminal Justice Statistics, 1995* (Washington, D.C.: Bureau of Justice Statistics, 1996), p. 183.
3. Francis T. Cullen and Karen E. Gilbert, *Reaffirming Rehabilitation* (Cincinnati: Anderson, 1982), p. 8.
4. American Friends Service Committee, *Struggle for Justice* (New York: Hill and Wang, 1971), p. 97.
5. M. Stanton Evans and Margaret Moore, *The Lawbreakers* (New Rochelle, N.Y.: Arlington House, 1968), p. 135.
6. James Q. Wilson, *Thinking About Crime* (New York: Basic Books, 1975), p. 172.
7. Ibid., p. 173.
8. Robert Martinson, "What Works: Questions and Answers About Prison Reform," *Public Interest* 35 (Spring 1974), pp. 22–54.
9. Martinson, p. 25.
10. American Friends Service Committee, *Struggle for Justice*, p. 144.
11. Donald Cressey, Foreword to Cullen and Gilbert, *Reaffirming Rehabilitation*.
12. Katherine Beckett, *Making Crime Pay* (Oxford: Oxford University Press, 1997), p. 91.
13. Nicholas Lemann, *The Promised Land* (New York: Knopf, 1991), p. 6.
14. Beckett, *Making Crime Pay*, pp. 31–32.
15. Ibid., p. 38.
16. Ibid., p. 26.
17. Dario Melossi, "Gazette of Morality and Social Whip: Punishment, Hegemony, and the Case of the USA, 1970–92," *Social and Legal Studies* 2 (1993), p. 266.

4—Crime as Politics

[Former President Jimmy] Carter cited inequities in the criminal justice system that often penalize blacks and other minority groups more than whites. He said that as a young Governor of Georgia, he and contemporaries like Reubin Askew in Florida and Dale Bumpers in Arkansas had "an intense competition" over who had the smallest prison population.

"Now it's totally opposite," Mr. Carter said. "Now the governors brag on how many prisons they've built and how many people they can keep in jail and for how long."

— *The New York Times*, April 28, 1997

In 1973, the year-end national federal and state prison population totaled 204,000, 4 percent higher than the year before. Few observations were made about this rise, relatively modest as it was. It was unusual in that it followed a 10 percent decline in the inmate population over the previous decade, but it was certainly not heralded as the inauguration of a new era in the policy of imprisonment.

In 1973, the "get tough" movement had not yet won the day. As previously noted, advocates for a moratorium on prison construction were becoming organized and gaining notable support from key professionals in the field; political calls for tougher sentencing policies were likewise finding receptive ears.

But the initial rise in prison populations in the 1970s was not itself a result of newly implemented "get tough" policies. In 1973, sentencing policies remained as they had been for many years; the population increase primarily resulted from the rise in crime rates.

Confronted with more arrests, convictions, and prison sentences, prison officials began to project the need for more space in which to house the growing number of offenders coming into the system. At the same time, changes in sentencing policy reflecting the growing consensus about the desirability of a more determinate system.

It soon became clear that the form these determinate sentencing policies would take was likely to be that of the harsh, fixed terms promoted by the "tough on crime" partisans. In 1973, the New York state legislature passed the so-called Rockefeller Drug Laws after the drug issue was given a high profile by Governor Nelson Rockefeller. At the time, these laws were the harshest in the nation, calling for mandatory prison terms for various narcotics offenses along with limits on plea bargaining. They have been described as policies that "set the stage in nearly every state for legislation in the following decades for new presumptive sentencing laws for drug crimes."[1]

Other states would adopt mandatory sentencing policies as well, generally for gun and drug offenses. In 1975, Massachusetts passed the Bartley – Fox Amendment, calling for a one-year mandatory prison term for unlawful carrying, but not necessarily use of, an unlicensed firearm. Michigan followed with the 1977 Felony Firearms Statute, which required a two-year mandatory prison sentence for use of a firearm in the course of committing a felony. Under the catchy slogan of "One with gun gets you two," billboard notices and other public announcements trumpeted the new law and its consequences.

Within just a few years of their adoption, each of these mandatory sentencing statutes were evaluated and found to be wanting, both in terms of their impact on crime control and in the distortions they produced within the criminal justice system. In New York, the Rockefeller Drug Laws led to fewer felony drug arrests and convictions but a greater likelihood of a prison term, and a longer one, for those who were convicted. The explanation for these patterns is that judges and prosecutors who felt that the mandatory terms were too harsh in some cases either declined to prosecute or found a means of convicting offenders under lesser statutes. For those offenders who were convicted, though, the mandatories ensured harsher sentences than prior to the law's adoption.

Similar findings were obtained in the evaluations of the Massachusetts gun law and the Michigan firearms statute. Practitioners used the discretion available to them to avoid having to impose overly harsh sanctions; in addition, in many cases trial rates and concomitant court time increased substantially among defendants hoping to avoid imposition of the mandatory term. In New York, for example, between 1973 and 1976 there was a tripling of drug felony dispositions resulting from trials.[2] These findings were well known in the field but, given the political nature of crime control measures, had little impact on future policy development.

While these mandatory sentencing laws were being adopted, other movements toward determinate sentencing were apace as well. An influential 1972 book by Judge Marvin Frankel called for the establishment of sentencing commissions as administrative agencies that would set general policy and guidelines on sentencing, with at least some distance from direct political concerns.[3] By 1979, Utah had adopted voluntary sentencing guidelines, and the following year Minnesota adopted guidelines with the explicit purpose of controlling the growth of the prison population through sentencing "tradeoffs." That is, if the guidelines commission wished to increase sentences for certain categories of violent offenses, it would also have to lower prison terms for some nonviolent offenders so as to not inexorably contribute to prison expansion. Other states rejected this approach and promulgated guidelines that have failed to have any impact on slowing the growth of the prison population.

At the national level, efforts were inaugurated in the late 1970s to change the nature of federal sentencing policy. This movement resulted from a variety of concerns. The federal criminal code was in many respects an outdated document: parts of it were inconsistent or irrelevant to modern circumstances. The movement was also influenced, though, by the growing interest in determinate sentencing and the new idea of a sentencing commission.

As a result, the unlikely partnership of Senators Ted Kennedy and Strom Thurmond, normally polar opposites in Congress, came together to co-sponsor a series of federal sentencing reform bills. An early version of the legislation, Senate Bill 1, contained a host of threats to civil liberties and labor rights. After much opposition developed, these were eventually scuttled, but the liberal–conservative coalescence of forces continued to pursue the goal of determinate sentencing.

Ultimately, this led to passage of the 1984 Sentencing Reform Act and its establishment of a federal sentencing commission. The guidelines developed by the commission went into effect in 1987, carrying a heavy presumption of imprisonment for most offenders and giving little regard for any mitigating circumstances involved in an offense. Within a few years of their adoption, the guidelines provoked widespread criticism and dissent from those charged with implementing them, leading sentencing scholar Michael Tonry to describe them as "the most controversial and disliked sentencing reform in U.S. history."[4]

While the sentencing policy changes of the 1970s were developing, the national political climate continued to shift to the right, which was reflected in increased public support for "tough on crime" policies. Finally, by 1980, the election of Ronald Reagan solidified this change of direction.

THE REAGAN/BUSH YEARS

The eight-year reign of Ronald Reagan was notable for its success in "re-inventing" the role of government, or lack thereof, in regard to social problems. Within the realm of justice policy, the change began at the top, with conservative Supreme Court appointments including Antonin Scalia and William Rehnquist as Chief Justice, and a consequent growing hostility to grievances brought by defendants and prisoners. At least as important, though, were the ideological shifts on crime policy promoted by the administration. With the complicity of Democrats in Congress, the Reagan administration succeeded in consolidating the "get tough" approach to crime control and institutionalizing a set of approaches that continue to shape the national response to crime.

The philosophical shift on crime policy promoted by the administration was in keeping with the administration's contention that "big government" was not the solution to societal problems, since individuals were responsible for their own destiny in this land of opportunity. In a 1982 speech on crime policy, Reagan contended that the American people

> utterly reject . . . utopian presumptions about human nature that see man as primarily a creature of his material environment. By changing this environment through expensive social programs, this philosophy holds that government can permanently change man and usher in an era of prosperity and virtue. In much the same way, individual wrongdoing is seen as the result of poor socioeconomic conditions or an underprivileged background. This philosophy suggests in short that there is crime or wrongdoing, and that society, not the individual, is to blame.[5]

In order to combat problems, therefore, punishment of the offender, rather than efforts to prevent the emergence of new offenders or to reform those who were apprehended, became the policy of choice.

Defining an appropriate role for the federal government to play in crime control, though, was a bit of a challenge for the Reagan administration. Most crime, after all, is locally based and prosecuted; fewer than 10 percent of all offenses fall under federal jurisdiction. Historically, the federal role in crime control has emphasized providing technical assistance to state and local governments, using the resources of agencies such as the FBI and the Drug Enforcement Administration, and prosecuting uniquely federal offenses, such as immigration and tax law violations.

One means of expanding the federal role in crime policy was by taking on the drug problem, thus offering intriguing political possibilities for an administration seeking to send a moral message and wanting to take visible action. If the administration wanted to deploy a "strong federal law enforcement capacity" in a "highly popular" manner, recommended Attorney General William French Smith, a federal war on drugs would fit the bill.[6]

The strategy of the new war on drugs involved several components. At the rhetorical level, it was led by first lady Nancy Reagan's "Just Say No" campaign designed to discourage youngsters from experimenting with drugs. Despite its lack of sophistication or relationship to any research in the field, as "sound bite" politics, the slogan clearly grabbed attention.

At the policy level, the inception of the drug war involved providing more resources to federal drug agencies and a greatly enhanced role for the federal court system in prosecuting drug offenses. Thus, in 1982, the administration and Congress authorized $125 million to establish twelve new regional drug task forces staffed by more than a thousand new FBI and DEA agents and federal prosecutors.

At the same time, the number of federal drug prosecutions began to increase dramatically. While federal prosecutions for all nondrug offenses increased by less than 4 percent from 1982 to 1988, drug prosecutions rose by 99 percent during this period.

Unlike street crimes such as burglary, robbery, or murder, which are almost always prosecuted at the local level, there is a great deal of discretion involved in how drug cases are charged. A drug offense may involve a violation of either federal or state law, and may or may not be of sufficient seriousness that it is deemed worthy of prosecution. Traditionally, federal prosecutors have taken on the prosecution of more complex and high-level offenses, under the assumption that the resources available to them are generally more abundant than those available to local prosecutors. The scale of the increase in drug prosecutions during the 1980s, though, was far greater than any actual rise in drug offenses; it reflected instead political directives to enhance these activities.

The primary elements of the drug war were in place by the early 1980s, but it was not until 1986 that the war would begin to explode in dramatic fashion. Beginning in 1984 and 1985, a new form of cocaine began to be seen in inner-city neighborhoods in Los Angeles, Miami, and New York; this mixture of cocaine powder, water, and baking soda, "crack," was sold in small, inexpensive units, and so it initially became a means of marketing a form of the more expensive powder cocaine to a low-income clientele.

As we shall see later, a media frenzy regarding the new drug developed by 1986, with much of the hysteria fueled by reports and information that later proved to be inaccurate. Then in June 1986, University of Maryland basketball star Len Bias died of a drug overdose, reportedly crack. Though the U.S. Sentencing Commission later concluded that there was no evidence that Bias in fact had been using crack, the Bias tragedy at the time became an instant national headline. The young and very talented athlete had just been drafted by the Boston Celtics of the NBA, home of House Speaker Tip O'Neill, and was virtually certain to have a very promising career ahead of him. Congress responded to this tragedy as it often does, by passing laws. Although there were virtually no hearings held or experts consulted, Congress moved to adopt a series of mandatory sentencing laws prescribing stiff mandatory prison terms for a variety of drug offenses. Ironically, the bipartisan legislation was passed just a year before the major overhaul of the federal sentencing system crafted by the United States Sentencing Commission was due to be implemented. The commission's guidelines, though criticized by many from a variety of perspectives, were at least an attempt by an independent body to establish a graduated scale of punishments for federal offenses. Now, without any acknowledgment of the impending guidelines, Congress superseded the work of the commission it had created.

By 1988, the Reagan administration and Congress continued the push to "get tough" on drugs. The vehicle this time was "The Anti-drug Abuse Act of 1988," which contained yet more mandatory sentencing laws among its hundreds of provisions. The Act also declared that it would be national policy to "create a Drug-Free America by 1995."[7] Needless to say, by 1995 there were few celebrations of a drug-free America or even evaluations of why this "national policy" had failed to achieve its goals.

However, the Reagan administration had succeeded in stoking the ideological fires for "tougher" crime policy, and this success would carry over into the administration of George Bush. In the final year of the Reagan presidency, Assistant Attorney General William Bradford Reynolds sent a memorandum to key leaders within the Justice Department, "A Strategy for the Remaining Months"; the memorandum proposed that the administration attempt to "polarize the debate" on a variety of public health and safety issues—drugs, AIDS, obscenity, prisons, and other issues.[8] Reynolds suggested that "we must not seek 'consensus,' we must confront . . . in ways designed to win the debate and further our agenda."

On the issue of prisons, Reynolds feared that while the demand for prison space would rise due to overcrowding, "so will the voices of those who say we need fewer prisons and more 'alternatives' to incarceration." This would clearly be unacceptable, and so in order "to polarize the issue we must attack those by name (such as Sen. Paul Simon) who take the other approach. . . . Overall, of course, we must make the case that public safety demands more prisons."

These themes clearly resonated with the managers of George Bush's 1988 election campaign. Although riding on the heels of Ronald Reagan's popularity, the campaign needed to boost the fortunes of a candidate who was hardly a great charismatic figure. As we now know, the late Lee Atwater convened his infamous focus groups to develop a "wedge" issue with which to confront candidate Michael Dukakis. The hapless and somewhat unstable Willie Horton, a convicted murderer who had committed a particularly vicious rape and attack after being released on a prison furlough, proved to be the perfect focal point of such a strategy. Aided by an inept Dukakis response on the issue of the death penalty in their nationally televised debate, Bush went on to claim victory as the image of this black killer flooded the airwaves.

Bush inherited a Justice Department intent on ensuring that the federal government play a leading role in promoting ever-harsher punitive policies on crime. This coordinated strategy employed various funding, research, and policy-making arms of the department in the service of a full-scale public relations campaign on behalf of enhanced prison construction. Such a campaign was admittedly not an easy task in some regards, since leading researchers in the field had doubted the wisdom of continued prison expansion for some time. Several national commissions composed of noted academics and practitioners had concluded that incarceration generally had modest impacts on deterring and incapacitating offenders.[9]

Indeed, back in 1983 the Reagan Justice Department had published a research briefing paper summarizing the state of knowledge about the crime control impact of a strategy of "collective incapacitation"—that is, punishing all offenders convicted of a certain offense with the same prison sentence. Under such a system, all second-time robbers might receive a five-year prison sentence. The paper concluded that "the most striking finding is that incapacitation does not appear to achieve large reductions in crime,"[10] but that these policies "can cause enormous increases in prison populations."[11]

The Justice Department was not to be deterred by these awkward findings, though. One of their own researchers, Edwin Zedlewski, a career statistician with the department, conducted an examination of the economic value of prison. In a 1987 report published by the department, "Making Confinement Decisions," Zedlewski calculated that incarcerating a single offender saved the taxpayers a staggering $405,000.[12] This finding, if accurate, would have represented a truly remarkable public policy success, one that should have encouraged state policymakers to proceed swiftly to build and fill prisons. Unfortunately, the study was probably one of the most flawed pieces of government-produced research ever published.

Zedlewski's statistical miscalculations were numerous, but the most significant was his estimate of the crime-reducing potential of incarceration. In order to derive his estimates in this regard, Zedlewski relied upon a survey of prison inmates in three states that had been conducted by the RAND Corporation, a Santa Monica–based research organization.[13] For incarcerated felony offenders, RAND researchers had calculated that the *average* offender had committed between 187 and 287 crimes in the year prior to his incarceration. This average, though, reflected crimes committed by a small number of very high-rate offenders. The median offending rate was a much more modest total of 15 crimes per year.

Zedlewski's estimate of the potential reduction in crime relied upon the average offending rate, and not the median, thereby vastly inflating the potential for lowering crime through incapacitation. Since the high-rate offenders are more likely to have been apprehended and incarcerated in most states, it is far more likely that expanding the prison population will result in the incarceration of offenders whose offending rates are much closer to the median. These and other errors were widely critiqued by a range of leading criminologists, including Franklin Zimring and Gordon Hawkins, who described the analysis as a case study of "compound catastrophic error."[14] Zimring and Hawkins, publishing in *Crime and Delinquency*, one of the leading journals in the field, demonstrated how, using Zedlewski's assumptions, the 237,000 increase in the number of prison inmates from 1977 to 1986 should have completely eliminated crime in the United States.

Within a year of its publication, the Zedlewski research had been roundly attacked by a host of leading academics and others. As early as January 1988, The Sentencing Project published a critical briefing paper that was reported on by one of the widely circulated professional newsletters in the field. By the fall of 1988, critiques by highly regarded scholars had appeared in other professional journals that were well known within the Justice Department.

These questioning voices were of little concern to the ideologues in the Justice Department, though. In July 1988, the Justice Department formally released the study to the news media, contending that "prisons appear to be good investments for reducing crime."[15] Since the report had been published a year earlier, one can only conclude that its "official" release in 1988 was a component of a strategy of a department that was attempting to "polarize the debate."

The report and its conclusions were then broadly disseminated under the leadership of Richard Abell, head of the Office of Justice Programs. This included publishing an article in *Policy Review*, the journal of the Heritage Foundation,[16] delivering a keynote address to a national symposium organized by the National Association of Counties, and sending a "Dear colleague" letter to criminal justice leaders nationally, with the admonition, "the choices are not easy—either build prisons or let convicted offenders back into our communities."[17]

As a campaign designed to use discredited research to deliver an ideological message, the department's efforts were quite successful. For years afterward, the familiar refrain of "saving $405,000 for every offender who is incarcerated" became a staple opening line for many members of Congress and state legislatures describing their approach to the problem. Frustrated academics and criminal justice professionals bemoaned the deception and dishonesty of the campaign, but their limited resources were little match for the federal government and its conservative allies.

The department was clearly on an ideological roll, but it had barely begun to reach its potential until the resignation of Attorney General Richard Thornburgh in 1991. His replacement, William Barr, Deputy Attorney General in the Justice Department, was determined to "hit the ground running" and leave his mark on public policy.

Barr quickly coined a sound bite to describe his approach to the crime problem—"more prisons or more crime." As a sound bite, it met all the criteria for a compelling call to arms. Short, catchy, and intuitively obvious to the layperson, the slogan served to draw in all but the most hardened ACLU supporter to the pro-prison camp. As a sound bite, of course, the chant hardly permitted any subtlety in the discussion. Thus, there was little regard for whether policy approaches other than building prisons might affect the crime rate, nor any discussion concerning whether there was *any* upper limit beyond which prison might prove ineffective, let alone inhumane.

Barr set out to make his mark quickly and provocatively. In his travels around the country, he compellingly laid out his agenda for harsher crime policies, augmenting this with publications and conferences. His 1992 publication, "Combating Violent Crime: 24 Recommendations to Strengthen Criminal Justice," became a popular document among the "get tough" crowd. Among its recommended policies were enhanced mandatory minimum penalties, building more prisons (the "morally right thing to do," as well as being cost-effective), "tough juvenile sanctions," and other measures.[18]

In April 1992, Barr's Justice Department organized a high-profile Washington event, the "Attorney General's Summit on Corrections: Expanding Capacity for Serious Offenders." Such summit meetings in Washington are hardly nonpartisan events in general, although this one pursued its ideological agenda with particular zeal. The invitation-only event attracted 300 state and local officials, many of whom left the meeting very critical of the limited room for discussion of policy options. The Nebraska Director of Corrections described the conference as "well-rehearsed and orchestrated," while Connecticut's Corrections Commissioner concluded that "this is a tired old message, with no recognition that it has already bankrupted the states."[19]

By the time of Barr's leaving office early in 1993 after just over a year as attorney general, he could be quite proud of his accomplishments. The "get tough" movement had benefitted from the largesse of the federal government through research, publications, and command of the political agenda, and the voices of dissent among practitioners or reformers had been suppressed or marginalized. The "war on drugs" was raging in full force:

drug arrests nationally exceeded one million a year, and harsher sentencing policies were being adopted across the country. The political and fiscal agenda of the Reagan and Bush administrations had been quite successful: between 1980 and 1993, federal spending on employment and training programs had been cut nearly in half, while corrections spending had increased by 521 percent.[20] If "getting tough" was the goal of these policies, the campaign was a great success. If cutting crime or investing tax dollars wisely was the goal, though, it would be difficult to point to much in the way of results. Given the political manipulation of the issues, though, it is unlikely that the higher reaches of the administration wasted much time in assessing the effectiveness of these policies on producing public safety.

THE CLINTON YEARS

And finally, and perhaps most importantly, we must do more to prevent crime through measures like community-based policing, the Police Corps, drug treatment, education, and job training.
— Candidate Bill Clinton, October 1992[21]

The most important accomplishment in every district is the passage of "three strikes and you're out". . . . No other accomplishment even comes close, suggesting that the agenda message should give a more central place to crime. Indeed, crime is an opportunity for Democrats.
— White House pollster Stanley Greenberg advising Democratic candidates, August 1994[22]

In 1992, candidate Bill Clinton reviewed the history of recent Democratic national campaigns. As a "new" Democrat, he calculated that traditional Democratic appeals to working people and the poor would be poorly received, given the importance of middle-class suburban voters. For this reason an approach to crime policy was a "no-brainer." Looking at the debacle of the Dukakis campaign, Clinton and his strategists concluded that no Democratic candidate should ever permit a Republican to be perceived as "tougher" on crime.

Thus, in early 1992, just weeks before the critical New Hampshire primary, candidate Clinton chose to fly home to Arkansas to oversee the execution of Ricky Ray Rector, a mentally impaired black man who had so little conception of what was about to happen to him that he asked that the dessert from his last meal be saved for him until the morning. After the execution, Clinton remarked, "I can be nicked on a lot, but no one can say I'm soft on crime."[23]

To be fair, candidate Clinton's policy prescriptions advocated a mixed approach to crime policy, one that did not exclusively focus on incarceration and the death penalty. His campaign speeches frequently described the need for drug treatment, along with his call for 100,000 new police to implement community policing.

The climate for such proposals was receptive in many regards. Despite the ideological zeal of the Reagan and Bush administrations in promoting expanded incarceration, significant changes were taking place in the field of criminal justice and opposition to the "lock 'em up" mentality was growing in some quarters. In the 1980s, spurred in part by John Hinckley's attack on Ronald Reagan, many law enforcement leaders nationally became convinced of the logic of gun control legislation and used their credibility and visibility to raise substantial political and public support for the Brady gun control bill. Among other criminal justice professionals, increasing calls were heard for a slowdown in prison growth and the need for a more balanced approach to crime control. The argument that "we can't build our way out of the prison overcrowding crisis," once the exclusive call of reformers, had become standard fare in the speeches of many corrections officials and even some state legislators as they came to recognize that the size of a given prison system was related at least as much to public policy choices as it was to crime rates. By 1992, over 600 criminal justice and elected officials nationally had come together to support the newly formed Campaign for an Effective Crime Policy in its "Call for a Rational Debate on Crime and Punishment."

The early 1990s also witnessed growing support for a variety of alternatives to incarceration. Having begun as modest efforts in the 1970s to divert primarily non-violent offenders from a prison term, these programs had now blossomed to the point where they were an integral part of many court systems. While many of these programs could not necessarily document their impact on prison populations, their presence in many communities helped to create a more receptive climate for consideration of a range of sentencing options other than incarceration.

Finally, the period was one in which growing attention was paid to the dramatic racial disparities within the criminal justice system. Several studies documenting the high rate of criminal justice control for young African American males had gained national attention. Bar groups, including the American Bar Association and a number of state court systems, established commissions to examine the causes and remedies for racial disparity in the criminal justice system. Congressional hearings on the issue further served to document the problem and to raise the level of public attention.

Elected as a centrist Democrat, Bill Clinton might not have raised significant expectations regarding the prospects for criminal justice reform had it not been for his bad luck with political appointments. Upon taking office, Clinton's first two nominees for Attorney General, Zoe Baird and Kimba Wood, were forced to withdraw due to public concerns over their hiring of illegal aliens as child-care providers. Neither of these candidates were necessarily expected to promote any dramatic shifts in criminal justice policy. Finally, Clinton gained Senate acceptance for his third choice, Miami prosecutor Janet Reno.

Reno's initial months in office were rather startling in terms of her public discussion of crime control. In contrast with her predecessor, William Barr, Reno quickly began delivering high-profile speeches around the country that consistently preached the message that "prenatal care is more important than prisons" in controlling crime. Whether or not this theme was developed in consultation with the White House (there are few indications that it was), the message and the messenger rapidly became very popular. Reno was portrayed as an honest, down-to-earth leader who cared about people. She was featured on the cover of *Time* magazine and quickly became one of the most popular figures in the administration. Rejecting conventional political wisdom on crime, Reno pursued her strong pro-prevention message. Far from being condemned as "soft on crime," public response to her message was very supportive.

On the policy front, Reno personally opposed the death penalty and also joined in with those criminal justice leaders who questioned the wisdom of mandatory sentencing. While not condemning it outright, she made clear in a number of statements that she was far from convinced that mandatory sentencing policies were fair or appropriate, and even left room for consideration of repeal.

Thus, the early months of 1993 represented a time of cautious optimism for criminal justice reform. After twenty years of prison-building frenzy, perhaps some policy initiatives designed to slow down the pace of growth and invest in a broader-based approach might finally find some appeal and political support. Less than a year later, though, this optimistic scenario had been transformed into a repressive criminal justice climate rivaling that of any time during the preceding twenty years.

No single factor explains the dramatic reversal of fortune for the forces of criminal justice reform. What occurred was the creation of a vicious cycle of reaction composed of political grandstanding, media sensationalism, and organized advocacy by "law and order" proponents. As each sector raised the level of attention devoted to harsh crime policies, others joined in and collectively raised the ante.

Electoral "messages" were a principal element in the changed climate. Several of the off-year 1993 elections were quickly interpreted by media and politicians as important "get tough" statements by the electorate. These included the victory of George Allen in the Virginia gubernatorial race, after campaigning on a pledge to abolish parole, and the defeat of New York City Mayor David Dinkins by former prosecutor Rudolph Giuliani, despite the fact that crime had declined under the Dinkins administration. Even though some of these races were decided by a margin of only several percentage points, political pundits defined them as important statements by the electorate on crime policy. On the West Coast, by a three-to-one margin voters in Washington state approved the nation's first "three strikes and you're out" proposal requiring life without parole for three violent felonies, aided in part by a contribution of $60,000 by the National Rifle Association to the initiative's proponents.

Media sensationalism accelerated the solidification of Clinton's "tough on crime" stance. Several high-profile crimes in 1993 contributed to public concern about crime and violence. These included, most notably, the abduction and murder of twelve-year-old Polly Klaas in Petaluma, California, the random shootings by a gunman on a Long Island Railroad commuter train, and the murder of the father of basketball star Michael Jordan. What these crimes had in common was that they were random in nature and had victims who were not beleaguered residents of the inner city. Regardless of the almost-infinitesimal odds of these occurrences, the message they communicated to middle-class suburbanites was that they, too, could be victimized by such violence.

Accompanying these atypical crimes was a surge of media reporting about crime. A study conducted by the Center for Media and Public Affairs found that television coverage of crime more than doubled from 1992 to 1993, while murder coverage tripled during the period, despite the fact that crime rates were essentially unchanged.[24]

The organized conservative movement contributed to the hostile climate toward reform during this time, as a host of right-wing think tanks and advocacy groups carried on the themes and arguments pursued by the Bush administration. Former

Attorney General William Barr founded the First Freedom Coalition, a small operation but one that served to provide convenient sound bites for journalists interested in "the other side" of the crime debate. Barr's report for the Justice Department, "Combating Violent Crime," was reprinted and distributed by the Heritage Foundation to state and local officials.

Other allies included the American Legislative Exchange Council, the "free-market" legislative alliance that began issuing "scorecards" on state criminal justice policies—essentially mail-merge reports on state crime and incarceration rates that promoted virtually identical policy recommendations regardless of a particular state's conditions.

The conservative climate was aided as well by new initiatives from the NRA. Concerned about growing public sentiment for gun control and the Brady bill in particular, the NRA made a major investment in a diversion strategy by forming the lobbying group CrimeStrike, around the slogan that "criminals cause crime."[25] Without any evidence, they promoted the idea that dramatic reductions in crime had been achieved as a result of the two-decade-long rise in incarceration.

Given this context, the Clinton administration was faced with a major decision on how to formulate crime policy. While candidate Clinton's campaign rhetoric had endorsed expanded drug treatment and community policing, he had also advocated a variety of punitive approaches, including support for the death penalty, boot camps, and other measures. As president, he still had to determine how to position the administration on this issue as interest was developing in Congress for some type of federal crime legislation.

Much of the decision-making in this area was the responsibility of Attorney General Reno. Despite criticism from some quarters, Reno's stock generally rose after the federal assault on the Branch Davidians at Waco in April 1993. Reno was viewed by many as both decisive and willing to accept responsibility, even though there was a tragic loss of lives. But in the months following, Reno's stature began to decline, as she faced criticism regarding her managerial skills. Major articles in the *New York Times* and the *Wall Street Journal* portrayed the Justice Department as adrift because of Reno's inability to delegate authority or make decisions.

In developing a crime bill strategy, the White House ordinarily might have relied on the attorney general—after all, this was her area of expertise, and her early months in office had demonstrated that she could rally public support for her ideas. Such a strategy could have permitted Reno to develop a crime policy that, if it had followed her earlier formulations, would have emphasized prevention, drug treatment, and other alternative approaches.

Whether due to concern over Reno's public image or her orientation on crime policy, the White House turned away from the Attorney General. Trying to "take the crime issue" away from Republicans, the administration eventually focused its attention on funding for more police, "three strikes," gun control, and increased spending on prisons and boot camps.

The retreat to traditional anticrime policies can be seen most clearly in the case of mandatory sentencing policies. For several years, an increasing drumbeat of criticism had been developing against federal mandatory minimum sentences in particular. A major study issued by the U.S. Sentencing Commission in 1991 documented the disparities and injustices caused by these policies, and assessed the widespread criticism of them by criminal justice personnel.[26] The federal judiciary, normally a fairly cautious body, developed a very vocal position on the issue: for example, all twelve judicial circuits issued statements opposing mandatory sentencing, and several prominent judges either resigned or refused to hear cases involving mandatory drug charges.

Early in her tenure, Janet Reno had expressed concern about mandatory sentencing, and subsequently formed a Justice Department working group to undertake a study designed to document the impact of federal mandatory sentences, particularly regarding low-level drug offenders. The study itself revealed disturbing evidence about the impact of public policy in this area. It found that more than a third (36 percent) of all incarcerated drug offenders were low-level offenders, characterized by limited criminal histories, the absence of violence in their offenses, and minimal roles in the drug trade.[27] This group of inmates constituted a fifth of the entire federal prison population, representing a substantial financial investment.

The report had been completed in August 1993, but was not released until February 1994. Had this study been issued in a timely manner, it could have played an important role in the national debate on the crime bill. Instead, the White House clearly made efforts to dilute any impact it might have had. According to the *New York Times*, Attorney General Reno "soon learned the White House game plan: never expose Clinton's right flank on crime."[28] After Deputy Attorney General Philip Heymann resigned in early 1994, he described how the report had been held up by the administration because it couldn't determine the proper "spin" to place on it. Media coverage of Heymann's remarks forced the administration to release the report, yet it did so in a manner designed to minimize any impact it might have — late on a Friday afternoon, thus guaranteeing that at most it would receive Saturday media coverage, the least significant news day of the week. While the report contained some potentially damaging information on mandatory sentencing, it was unattractively designed and, most significantly, contained no recommendations to Congress regarding action that could be taken.

By this time, of course, most of the damage had already been done. Nothing remotely resembling mandatory sentencing repeal was contained in the leading Democratic and Republican crime bills. Several versions of a "safety valve" designed to ameliorate the impact of mandetory sentences on a relatively modest number of low-level drug offenders had been incorporated into the House and Senate crime proposals, even as new additional mandatories were added to the Senate bill. On the critical issue of whether the safety valve should apply retroactively to inmates already serving a prison term, the Justice Department took the position that doing so would involve an inordinate amount of paperwork and was therefore unfeasible.

Reno's apparent "softness" on crime led the White House to seek assurance that the Justice Department would stay in line with the administration's crime policy; in the words of a senior White House official, "to pull things together and get the department to be real."[29] Early in 1994, therefore, the White House recommended the appointment of Ron Klain as counselor to Reno, with an initial responsibility of coordinating the effort to pass the crime bill. Klain was a logical choice for a pragmatic administration; he had drafted much of the crime bill while serving as chief counsel to the Senate Judiciary Committee, and subsequently serving in the White House counsel's office.

In addition to such policy choices as deciding that the administration should be "aggressively neutral" in its position on the Racial Justice Act (which would have challenged racial disparity in the imposition of the death penalty), Klain's biggest accomplishment was recruitment of Reno for the administration's approach. Reno didn't favor the Clinton proposal for 100,000 new police, said Klain, "until we sent her out on a crime bill trip . . . and she came back saying, 'You know what? Community policing works!'" He added: "You look at her speeches since the crime bill—they're all about the crime bill. And the crime bill reflects her whole agenda."[30]

Once the stage was set for a crime bill that echoed the themes coming out of the White House, it was politics as usual. The Clinton administration, attempting to show that it too could be "tough," quickly endorsed the idea of a federal "three strikes and you're out" law after its passage by voters in Washington state in November 1993. The proposal was even incorporated into the president's 1994 State of the Union address, where it was greeted enthusiastically on both sides of the aisle.

In an effort to respond to concerns about the proposal being too broad in scope, the administration presented a relatively narrow bill, primarily covering violent offenses. In the heated political climate in Congress, though, conservatives were hardly appeased by such a modest proposal. Congressional committees quickly broadened the proposal by incorporating drug offenses.

Congress ultimately passed a six-year $30 billion legislative package heavily weighted toward law enforcement and incarceration. Almost $8 billion of the total funding was directed toward prison construction, accompanied by incentives for states to toughen penalty structures in order to qualify for funding. Another $1.8 billion was allocated to the incarceration of illegal aliens, and $8.8 billion for policing. In addition to the funding provisions, the legislation expanded the federal death penalty, eliminated the awarding of Pell grants for higher education to prisoners, and created fiscal incentives for states to increase prison terms through its "truth in sentencing" provisions.

Former Deputy Attorney General Philip Heymann described the Clinton approach as "the most careful political calculation, with absolutely sublime indifference to the real nature of the problem."[31] In regard to the popular policing initiative, Heymann noted that violent crime was not a growing problem in most parts of the country, but that granting funding for more police was popular in all congressional districts. Violence, Heymann noted, "is a problem that is concentrated within very clearly defined geographic boundaries. And the president is going to spread cops into every suburb in the country."

The final legislation included $7 billion in funding for a range of prevention programs as well, enabling congressional leaders to tout the bill's balanced approach. What went unsaid, though, was the critical role played by the Congressional Black Caucus in this regard. Initially faced with Democratic and Republican crime bills that contained few funds for prevention, the caucus developed its own crime legislation, emphasizing prevention and treatment, along with proposals to ensure racial fairness in the justice system. The bill received favorable commentary from the *Washington Post* and was the subject of two days of hearings in the House Judiciary Subcommittee on Crime.

In order to win over the substantial block of Democratic votes in the House represented by the caucus, legislative leaders incorporated many of the funding recommendations of the caucus into the final bill. Even with these additions, the caucus ultimately split on support for the bill, with about half its members voting against the legislation due to its imbalance in funding and failure to incorporate provisions of the Racial Justice Act, which would have broadened the scope of permissible challenges regarding racial bias in imposition of the death penalty.

As an overall strategy, the White House and its Democratic allies in Congress had argued that what was needed in crime policy was a mixture of punishment and prevention. This is hard to quarrel with in the abstract, but the problem with this strategy is that by 1994, there was *not* in fact an equal need to expand both punishment and prevention. Twenty years of "get tough" policies along with declining support for social welfare programs had created a bloated prison system and contributed to a decaying urban economy and community. By failing to directly challenge the tendency toward prison construction or to face down the assumptions upon which it was based, the advocacy of punishment mixed with prevention actually assisted the further establishment of the "tough on crime" strategy. Whether the Clinton administration could have successfully provided an alternative crime control strategy and succeeded politically is not clear; it is clear, though, that the administration never even tried.

NOTES

1. Jeffrey Fagan, "Crack in Context: Myths and Realities From America's Latest Drug Epidemic," paper presented at conference on The Crack Decade: Research Perspectives and Lessons Learned, National Institute of Justice, Baltimore, November 5, 1997, p. 6.

2. Michael Tonry, *Sentencing Matters* (New York: Oxford University Press, 1995), pp. 152–59.
3. Marvin Frankel, *Criminal Sentences: Law Without Order* (New York: Hill and Wang, 1972).
4. Tonry, *Sentencing Matters*, p. 72.
5. Ronald Reagan, "Remarks Announcing Federal Initiatives Against Drug Trafficking and Organized Crime," Oct. 14, 1982, cited in Dan Baum, *Smoke and Mirrors: The War on Drugs and the Politics of Failure* (Boston: Little, Brown, 1996), pp. 170–71.
6. Cited in Baum, *Smoke and Mirrors*, p. 140.
7. Office of National Drug Control Policy, *National Drug Control Strategy* (Washington, D.C.: Office of National Drug Control Policy, 1989), p. 9.
8. William Bradford Reynolds, "Memorandum for Heads of Department Components," Department of Justice, Feb. 22, 1988.
9. See, for example, Alfred Blumstein, Jacqueline Cohen, and Daniel Nagin, *Deterrence and Incapacitation: Estimating the Effects of Criminal Sanctions on Crime Rates* (Washington, D.C.: National Academy Press, 1978).
10. Jacqueline Cohen, *Incapacitating Criminals: Recent Research Findings* (Washington, D.C.: National Institute of Justice, December 1983), p. 3.
11. Ibid., p. 5.
12. Edwin W. Zedlewski, *Making Confinement Decisions* (Washington, D.C.: National Institute of Justice, July 1987).
13. Jan Chaiken and Marcia Chaiken, *Varieties of Criminal Behavior* (Santa Monica, Calif.: RAND Corporation, 1982).
14. Franklin Zimring and Gordon Hawkins, "The New Mathematics of Imprisonment," *Crime and Delinquency* 34 (Oct. 1988), p. 431.
15. Press release, Department of Justice, July 3, 1988.
16. Richard B. Abell, "Beyond Willie Horton: The Battle of the Prison Bulge," *Policy Review* (Winter 1989), pp. 32–35.
17. Richard B. Abell, Assistant Attorney General, "Dear Criminal Justice Colleague," Jan. 19, 1989.
18. William Barr, *Combating Violent Crime: 24 Recommendations to Strengthen Criminal Justice* (Washington, D.C.: Department of Justice, 1992).
19. *Criminal Justice Newsletter*, April 1, 1992, p. 2.
20. Elliott Currie, *Crime and Punishment in America* (New York: Metropolitan Books, 1998), p. 31.
21. "Bush v. Clinton: The Candidates on Legal Issues," *ABA Journal* (Oct. 1992), p. 61.
22. Richard L. Berke, "Advice for Democrats in Fall: Don't Be Too Close to Clinton," *New York Times*, 5 Aug. 1994, p. A1.
23. Michael Kramer, "Frying Them Isn't the Answer," *Time*, 14 March 1994, p. 32.
24. "Crime Down, Media Crime Coverage Up," *Overcrowded Times* (April 1994), p. 7.
25. NRA CrimeStrike, *The Case for Building More Prisons* (Washington, D.C.: NRA CrimeStrike, 1994).
26. United States Sentencing Commission, *Mandatory Minimum Penalties in the Federal Criminal Justice System* (Washington, D.C.: United States Sentencing Commission, Aug. 1991).

27. Department of Justice, *An Analysis of Non-violent Drug Offenders with Minimal Criminal Histories* (Washington, D.C.: Department of Justice, Feb. 4, 1994).

28. Jeffrey Goldberg, "What Is Janet Reno Thinking?" *New York Times Magazine*, July 6, 1997, p. 21.

29. Ruth Shalit, "The Kids Are Alright," *New Republic* (July 18 – 25, 1994), pp. 23 – 31.

30. Ibid., p. 25.

31. David Johnston and Tim Weiner, "Seizing the Crime Issue as His Own," *New York Times*, Aug. 1, 1996.

5—The Prison-crime Connection

As we have noted, the quarter-century-long prison buildup that resulted in a sextupling of the prison population is unprecedented in American history, and perhaps that of any modern nation using this institution as a means of crime control. The costs of this buildup, both in fiscal and human terms, have been substantial, with corrections spending now approaching $40 billion a year nationally.

Much discussion, not to mention hyperbole, has taken place in recent years regarding the effect of the prison population increase on the crime rate. To the extent that incarceration is viewed as a natural response to crime, this would appear to be a reasonable relationship to examine. Before assessing this relationship, though, consider for a moment the larger context in which the question is posed. Locking up a convicted offender may indeed have some impact on crime. The fact that Charles Manson spends his years in a prison cell no doubt has reduced the number of additional persons he might have victimized. But most inmates are not of the Manson variety. Over half of all state and federal prison inmates are currently serving time for a nonviolent drug or property offense. While many of these offenders have had prior criminal convictions, the policy decision regarding their sentencing involves a consideration of whether spending $20,000 a year to incarcerate them is the wisest course of action. The alternative is not to do nothing but, rather, to explore whether some combination of community supervision, victim restitution, required treatment, and other conditions would more effectively respond to the needs of both victim and offender.

While imprisonment may have some impact on crime, either by incapacitating offenders for a period of time or by deterring inmates or potential offenders, it is hardly the only social policy option that may influence crime rates. What might other measures look like? High school graduation rates have been inching upwards in recent years. Might this have an impact on crime, either by making young graduates more employable or increasing their self-esteem? Divorce in the United States is far more common than a generation ago, as are single-parent families. How do these factors affect crime rates? How does this compare with the experience in other nations? What has been the impact of raising the minimum wage, or the advent of NAFTA, or community policing, or a variety of other social and economic changes?

Some of these factors have been examined in detail by researchers, while others have received less attention. The point is that they illustrate the complexity of understanding why crime rates might rise or fall over a period of time. Our exploration of the relationship between incarceration and crime needs to be understood in this larger context.

From the vantage point of the late 1990s, one might conclude, as have many political leaders, that prison is "working." After all, both overall crime rates and violent crime rates began a steady decline in 1992, coinciding with a period in which the prison population was steadily rising—ergo, there must be some relationship. However, if we examine a broader time period, beginning just prior to the prison buildup that began in the 1970s, the picture gets cloudy. As we can see for the 25-year period displayed in Figure 5-1, there are essentially four distinct periods of rise and fall in crime rates.[1] (In the figure, violent crime rates are multiplied by a factor of ten so that trends can be discerned on this scale.) Overall crime rates generally rose in the 1970s, then declined from 1980 to 1984, increased again from 1984 to 1991, and then declined through 1995. With only minor exceptions, violent crime rates have followed this pattern as well. Each of these phases, of course, occurred during a time when the prison population was continuously rising. Thus, a steadily increasing prison population has twice coincided with periods of increase in crime and twice with declines in crime.

The fact that the relationships are inconsistent does not mean

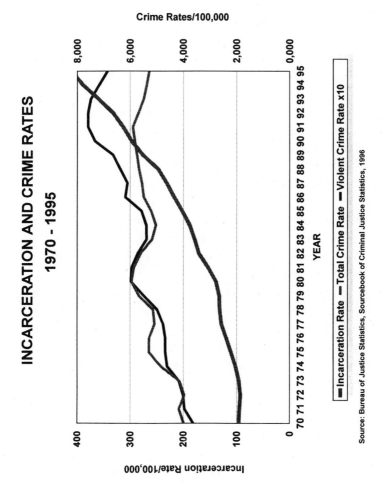

Figure 5-1
Incarceration and Crime Rates, 1970–1995

Source: Bureau of Justice Statistics, *Sourcebook of Criminal Justice Statistics,* 1996

that rising imprisonment had *no* impact on crime, but neither does it lend itself to a statement that incarceration had an unambiguously positive impact in this area. What is critical to note here as well is the scope of the changes being discussed—the unprecedented 328 percent increase in the rate of incarceration from 1970 to 1995. Property crime rates finally reached a 20-year low in 1995, but were still higher than in 1970 before the prison buildup began; and violent crime, with the exception of murder, was still consistently higher than the 1970 rate.

The decline in murder is not inconsequential, of course, and deserves close scrutiny. By 1995, national murder rates had declined by 20 percent to 8.2 per 100,000 population from a peak of 10.2 per 100,000 in 1980, a significant decline (and continued to decline to 6.8 per 100,000 in 1997). Yet looking again at the 1970–95 period, we find that the murder rate in 1995 was essentially the same as the rate of 8.3 per 100,000 in 1970. Thus, the best that can be said about changes in homicide is that these rates were *no worse* in 1995 than in 1970 despite the addition of nearly one million prison inmates.

Further, as we see from Table 5-2, one's risk of being murdered is very dependent on one's place of residence. In general, U.S. cities became less safe during this 25-year period. Sixteen of the 20 largest U.S. cities registered increases in murder rates during this time, with ten of these displaying a rise of 50 percent or more.

Overall, the murder rate has declined, and that is a welcome development. Whether much or most of this decline is attributable to increased incarceration, though, is not at all clear.

A critical issue in this regard concerns differing trends in homicide rates among juveniles and adults. From 1984 to 1993, for example, homicide rates among white males in the 14–17 age group doubled from 6.9 per 100,000 to 14.4 per 100,000, while for black males, the rate more than quadrupled, increasing from 33.4 to 151.6 per 100,000. For males 25 and over, though, homicide rates for both blacks and whites declined by more than 20 percent. Overall, 14–17-year-old males constituted 6.3 percent

Table 5-1

Murder Rates (per 100,000) for the 20 Largest Cities
1970–95

| City* | 1970 | | 1995 | | % Change in Rate |
	Number	Rate	Number	Rate	1970–95
New York	1117	14.2	1177	16.1	+13.4
Los Angeles	395	14.0	849	24.5	+75.0
Chicago	810	24.1	824	30.0	+24.5
Houston	289	23.5	316	18.2	−22.6
Philadelphia	352	18.1	432	28.2	+55.8
San Diego	32	4.6	91	7.9	+71.7
Phoenix	63	10.8	214	19.7	+82.4
Dallas	242	28.7	276	26.5	−7.7
San Antonio	73	11.2	142	14.2	+26.8
Detroit	495	32.8	475	47.6	+45.1
San Jose	12	2.7	38	4.6	+70.4
Indianapolis**	60	11.8	99	12.8	+8.5
San Francisco	108	15.1	99	13.4	−11.3

Table 5-1 (*continued*)

Murder Rates (per 100,000) for the 20 Largest Cities
1970–95

City*	1970		1995		% Change in Rate 1970–95
	Number	Rate	Number	Rate	
Baltimore	231	25.6	325	45.6	+78.1
Jacksonville	95	18.6	86	12.7	-31.7
Columbus	47	8.7	77	12.1	+39.1
Milwaukee	50	7.0	138	22.2	+217.1
Memphis	92	14.8	181	29.0	+95.9
El Paso	13	4.0	37	6.3	+57.5
Washington	221	29.2	360	65.0	+122.6

*Cities listed by population (1995) in descending order.

**Indianapolis figures are based on combined reporting for both the city of Indianapolis and Marion County.

Source: FBI homicide data provided to the author

of homicide offenders in the mid-1980s; this proportion doubled to 13 percent by the early 1990s.[2] By the mid-1990s, though, the juvenile murder rates began to drop precipitously. Between 1994 and 1995, juvenile homicides dropped 17 percent, with the bulk of this decline occurring among black males.[3]

The differing trends in juvenile and adult violence are significant because juveniles are essentially unaffected by the dramatic growth of the adult prison population. While more adult offenders were incapacitated in prison during this period, and therefore unable to commit crimes while locked up, this did not generally apply to juveniles. Therefore, whatever combination of circumstances contributed first to the rise and then to the decline of the juvenile homicide rate, the prison buildup was not one of these factors.

Other factors that may influence trends in this area include what has been described as an "attrition of the at-risk population."[4] This refers to the fact that the low-income minorities who are disproportionately murder victims and offenders have suffered high death rates in recent years from a variety of factors—violence, AIDS, accidents, and various preventable illnesses. In comparison to the homicide rate for black men aged 15–24 that reached 167 per 100,000 in 1993, for example, deaths for black males ages 25–34 from HIV infection reached 117 per 100,000. A study of young black men in Philadelphia over the years 1987–90 found that 40 percent had had at least one emergency room visit for a serious violent assault.[5]

Looking at violent crime overall, a number of studies have attempted to quantify the impact that rising imprisonment has had on these rates. The National Research Council of the National Academy of Sciences has estimated the impact of imprisonment on violent crime rates and concluded that the tripling of time served per violent crime from 1975 to 1989 had "very little" impact; it recommended that "*preventive* strategies may be as important as criminal justice *responses* to violence."[6] Similar findings have been seen in other nations. In a report for the

Home Office in the United Kingdom, analysts concluded that a 25 percent rise in the prison population would result in a 1 percent decline in overall crime rates.[7]

Other U.S. studies have tended to show that, to the extent that prison has any impact on crime, it is more likely to be observed in rates of property crime. An assessment of the incapacitating impact of the addition of more than 100,000 offenders to California's prisons and jails during the decade of the 1980s, for example, concluded that the bulk of the crime that may have been prevented through incarceration was concentrated in burglary—although even here the results were expressed with caution. Since most of the burglary decline was among juveniles, whereas the incarceration increase primarily affected adults, it is not clear how direct this relationship may have been.[8]

At the national level, the most significant area of change in crime rates for the period 1980–95 has also been in the area of burglary. As we can see in Table 5-2, although violent crime rates rose by 15 percent during this period, crime rates overall declined by 11 percent and property crime was down by 14 percent, The decline in burglary was the most substantial by far, falling by 41 percent, and accounting for fully 92 percent of the decline in property crime in this fifteen-year period.

To what extent, then, can we conclusively attribute this decline in burglary to increased incarceration? An examination of changes in the composition of the prison population for the years 1980–95 does not suggest that an increase in the number of imprisoned burglars was necessarily the primary factor at work. As Table 5-2 shows, during this period the overall number of state prison inmates rose by 234 percent, violent offenders by 168 percent, property offenders by 158 percent, and burglars by 114 percent. Thus, we see relatively modest changes in crimes rates for nonburglary offenses despite substantial increases in imprisonment, but a considerable decline in the burglary rate despite a lower rate of increase in the number of incarcerated burglars. This does not suggest that the imprison-

Table 5-2

Crime Rates and Incarceration, 1980–95

Crime	Rate per 100,000		% Change	% Change in State Prisoners
	1980	1995	1980–1995	1980–1995
All	5950	5278	–11%	+234%
Violent	597	685	+15%	+168%
Property	5353	4593	–14%	+158%
Burglary	1684	988	–41%	+114%

Sources: FBI Uniform Crime Reports 1995; Bureau of Justice Statistics, *Corrections Populations in the United States, 1994 and 1995*

ment of more burglars had no effect, but it should cause us to look to other factors that may provide a more full interpretation.

In looking at other possible explanations, we find that a certain and perhaps substantial portion of the burglaries may have been replaced by other kinds of criminal activity—most notably, drug crimes. The difficulty in quantifying this precisely relates to the way in which crime is measured. When we speak of the "crime rate," official measures refer to the FBI's annual Uniform Crime Reports, a national survey of eight crimes— murder, rape, robbery, aggravated assault, burglary, larceny, auto theft, and arson. These are among the most serious and common of crimes, at least of those which can be measured. "Victimless" crimes, though, cannot be accounted for by any police agency. So, personal drug use or drug sales, or gambling or consensual vice affairs do not result in a victim who reports such crimes to the police.

While there is no means of knowing exactly how many drug crimes were committed during the 1980s, evidence suggests that there may have been significant increases in many cities. Even though casual drug use had been declining since 1979, an increasing proportion of total drug consumption consisted of hard-core drug users, whose numbers had not declined. The irony of these trends is that the decline in casual use, primarily among middle-class users, predated the stepped-up pace of the drug war and was not a result of increased law enforcement efforts. Rather, these declines paralleled declines in other unhealthy lifestyle choices, such as cigarette and alcohol consumption, and can be seen as part of a broader trend toward healthier lifestyles. Hard-core users, though, who were disproportionately low-income, registered no declines in overall use despite being more likely to be subjected to arrest and prosecution.

As crack cocaine made its entry into urban areas beginning in the mid-1980s, new opportunities arose to make money quickly by becoming a street-level seller. While drug arrest rates are not necessarily a direct indicator of drug activity (certainly less so than for offenses such as murder or armed robbery), they nearly doubled from 1980 to 1990, an indicator of a potential increase in these activities.

In looking at the possible displacement of burglary to drug-selling, contrast the two crimes as a means of making money. Burglary involves entering a home illegally, never being certain whether the occupant is home or might even be armed. If small items such as cash or jewelry are not readily apparent, burglary requires stealing bulkier items such as televisions and sound systems, as well as having ready transportation for them. These must then be fenced to be turned into cash at a small fraction of the actual value.

Drug-selling, on the other hand, is much simpler in most respects. All it requires is a willing supplier and a vacant street corner. Transactions are completed in cash with no middleman. Selling drugs is not without its dangers, of course, either from rival drug dealers or the police; but in comparison to burglary it has a number of advantages for the potential offender. At least to a certain extent, the burglar of the 1980s may have become the drug seller of the 1990s.

Beginning in the mid-1980s, burglaries may have also been displaced to robberies as well. While burglary and robbery rates had moved in parallel fashion for about ten years, robbery rates began to increase in 1985 and continued to do so through the early 1990s, while burglary was steadily declining. For a drug addict seeking to obtain money to buy drugs, robbery may prove to be a quicker means of obtaining cash than burglary.

What we see overall in looking at crime rates over the 25-year period of rising incarceration is no dramatic decline, despite the unprecedented increase in the number of prisoners. In the following chapter, we will look at some of the reasons why this limited impact should have been expected, but for now one issue deserves focus.

If the number of inmates rose so steeply for a period of 25 years, yet crime rates did not decline very much, then either more people were committing crimes or those who were committing crimes committed them more frequently. In either case, this suggests that whatever combination of family, social, or economic factors leads individuals to crime must have become worse over time. Some would contend that the primary culprit was the deindustrialization of many cities, others that the rise of single-parent families was to blame. Whatever the mix of factors and regardless of whether one prefers the liberal or conservative explanation, the increased prison-building did not dramatically affect this growing propensity for criminal activities.

At least one influential commentator, though, is ready to offer a proposal for addressing some of these issues through changes in the prison system. Michael Block, an economist at the University of Arizona, contends in an article published by the National Institute of Justice that prison has not achieved its maximum capacity to deter crime.[9] Writing as only an economist can, Block describes how the "disincentive effect of imprisonment policy" has been limited in recent years due to the impact of prison litigation, which has reduced the ability of prison officials to increase the "severity" of punishment. He concludes that "policy initiatives aimed at increasing the unpleasantness of prison life would likely be a cost-effective method of fighting crime."[10]

"Increasing the unpleasantness of prison life" as a crime policy—what might this mean? Block does not offer specific recommendations, but some examples that come to mind are the conditions that prevailed in many prisons prior to the successful litigation that Block questions. As described in the professional journal of the American Correctional Association, these included the following:

—in one prison, inmates were punished by being forced to consume milk of magnesia, being handcuffed to a fence for long periods, and being shot at or around to keep them moving;
—another prison allowed unsupervised inmates to work in a prison medical unit, taking X-rays, giving injections, and doing suturing and minor surgery;

—yet another institution placed naked inmates in "strip cells," whose walls were caked with the body waste of previous inhabitants.[11]

Block does not necessarily endorse these types of "unpleasant" prison environments, but other policymakers in recent years have proposed, and sometimes implemented, chain gangs, whippings, and other methods of punishments from what we once had thought was a bygone era. Even among more reasonable analysts and policymakers, though, one may hear calls for a *slowing* of growth of the prison system, but rarely are any proposals offered for actually *reducing* the size of the prison population. An attitude of complacency has pervaded public policy discussion in this arena, whereby a record rate of imprisonment is either actively encouraged or passively accepted. Moreover, barring major policy shifts in the near future, the cumulative impact of such policies as mandatory sentencing, "truth in sentencing," and "three strikes and you're out" is likely to exacerbate the pressure to continue building new prisons.

These policies might be justifiable if there were great public acclaim for their success in controlling crime; but despite significant declines in crime in the 1990s, public opinion polls still demonstrate substantial concern about crime and violence. A 1997 Harris poll, for example, found that 67 percent of U.S. citizens thought that violent crime was increasing, while a Time/CNN poll the same year showed that half the public believed crime would be worse in their communities by the year 2000.[12]

In trying to make sense of the contradiction between falling rates of crime and public misinformation and pessimism on these issues, several possible explanations come to mind. Clearly, the ongoing barrage of media depictions of violence, which we shall explore in detail later, is one possible culprit. Along with this, though, has been the relative absence of alternative approaches to fighting crime in policy discussions. This void is not due to a lack of information or analysis. A number of studies published in recent years have documented the beneficial effects of nonprison options in reducing crime. A 1997 RAND study examined the relative benefits derived from spending an additional $1 million to cut drug consumption and drug-related crime through different policy interventions. The analysts concluded that spending the funds on reducing drug consumption through drug treatment would reduce serious crimes 15 times more effectively than incapacitating offenders by funding more mandatory prison terms.[13] Although this and other studies are well known in the field of criminal justice, their conclusions and recommendations are too often overshadowed in the political zeal to promote ever-harsher sentencing policies.

It remains true, of course, that imprisonment may seek to serve purposes other than crime reduction. Punishment of an offense has historically been a goal of sentencing intended to demonstrate society's condemnation of illegal behavior. Even if little is expected in the way of reducing crime by incarcerating a particular offender, there are occasions under which a prison sentence may be viewed as appropriate. Even though punishment has come to be all but equated with incarceration, any deprivation of liberty can be considered a form of punishment. Sentencing alternatives that might meet the punishment goals of the system while providing community-based services are forced to compete for dollars and attention with the growing prison complex.

No discussion of crime rates in recent years is complete, of course, without an examination of the dramatic decline of crime in New York City in the 1990s. As is well known, murder rates there have plummeted in recent years, dropping from 2,245 homicides in 1990 to 1,177 by 1995, a number comparable to that of the 1960s. This is welcome news indeed for all New Yorkers, and particularly for those in high-crime areas.

We should note that the 48 percent drop in murders from 1990 to 1995 followed a sharp rise in the five-year period of 1985 to 1990, when murders increased by 62 percent from 1,384 to

2,245, a record high. The decline came after an atypical peak year—one that, as we shall see, probably reflected much of the drug-related violence of the late 1980s.

New York's Police Department, along with Mayor Giuliani, has claimed credit for the crime drops, attributing it to their emphasis on aggressively addressing "quality of life" crimes and by intensive management efforts to confront high-crime areas with targeted enforcement strategies. To what extent, though, has the increased use of imprisonment been a factor in the reductions in New York crime?

Let's assume that if police make more arrests and lock up more offenders, then the incapacitating effect of higher prison and jail populations could ameliorate crime rates. Figure 5-2 shows changes in the jail population in New York City and the prison population for New York State (a majority of whose inmates are from New York City) for the period 1990–95. During this time, rates of violent crime declined by 34 percent and property crime by 39 percent in New York, a far steeper drop than national changes.

In looking at the use of incarceration, what we see is that the state prison population increase was significantly below that experienced nationally, and that the city's jail population actually declined somewhat during this period, compared to a national rise of 25 percent. If increased imprisonment is the answer to our crime problem, this has not been the secret of success in New York.

It is likely that the policing changes initiated under Police Chief William Bratton, particularly the problem-oriented strategies that focused on neighborhood-specific problems, were responsible in part for the lowered crime rates in the 1990s. Other factors that coincided with these changes, though, appear to contribute to the explanation as well.

To begin with, not only was crime declining in all parts of the nation in the first half of the 1990s, but it was dropping even more rapidly in the New York metropolitan area as a whole. From 1990 to 1995, as the rate of violent crime was declining by

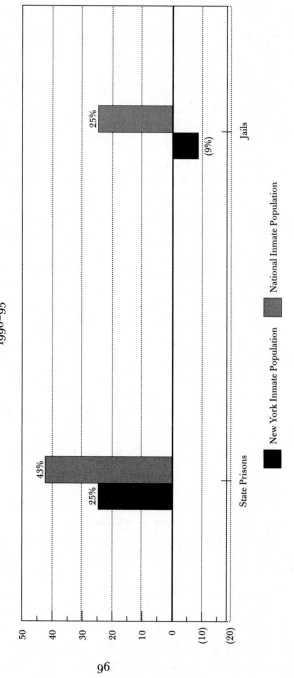

Figure 5-2

Increase in Incarceration
New York City and National
1990–95

50

40

30

20

10

0

(10)

(20)

43%

25%

25%

(9%)

State Prisons

Jails

■ New York Inmate Population   ▨ National Inmate Population

34 percent in New York City, the national decline was just 6.5 percent. Yet the drop in the metropolitan region of New York (excluding New York City) was 15 percent, considerably greater than the national average.[14] Thus, whatever strategic successes were enjoyed by the police department appear to have built on other regional factors working in their favor.

Changes in both the drug trade and drug use in New York may have also contributed to an exaggerated impact compared to other cities. Since a substantial portion of murders are drug-related (some studies estimate it to be as high as half[15]), any changes in drug markets and activities will often spark changes in homicide rates as well.

Research on crack cocaine in particular shows the beneficial impact for New York City of changes in crack use that began in the late 1980s. Just as New York was one of the first cities to experience the surge in crack use, so was it a leader in its decline. An analysis of trends in crack use published by the National Institute of Justice (NIJ) demonstrated that, particularly among young people, crack and cocaine use declined precipitously in the 1990s. Among youthful arrestees in Manhattan, for example, the rate of use declined from 70 percent in 1988 to 22 percent by 1996.[16]

While law enforcement efforts and the increased incarceration of drug offenders no doubt had some effect on crack use (though, again, much more modest than many of its proponents claimed), it also appears that a significant explanation for the reduced rates may be due to the "younger sibling" effect. This refers to the fact that the decline in crack use is due more to younger people not initiating use of the drug, and less so to older users cutting back on consumption. As children growing up a decade ago witnessed the devastation that crack brought to their older brothers and sisters, they were turned off by the drug. In contrast, the NIJ report concluded that "tougher sanctions appeared to have no major deterrent effect."[17]

A final note on crime control regards the long-term impacts

of various models of policing. To the extent that the Bratton–
Giuliani model involves a more aggressive and at times in-
timidating use of police force, it contrasts sharply with
developments in community policing in many other cities. Perhaps the sharpest contrast with New York can be seen in San
Diego, which instituted a far-reaching community policing effort during the past decade. This involved creating police–
community problem-solving partnerships, as opposed to the
New York strategy, which emphasized aggressive enforcement
of low-level offenses. The results are quite revealing. Both cities
experienced a 54 percent decline in homicides for the period
1991–96. In San Diego, where law enforcement focused on fos-
tering community trust rather than increasing arrests, the number of arrests declined by 15 percent from 1993 to 1996. In
contrast, overall arrests in New York rose by 23 percent during
this period and misdemeanor drug arrests, by 97 percent.[18]

The problem with aggressively enforcing "quality of life"
crimes and lower-level offenses is that it not only ignores the
community as a partner in crime-fighting strategies but often
heightens police–community tensions. This is exactly what has
taken place in New York, where the number of citizen complaints filed with the city's Civilian Complaint Review Board
rose more than 60 percent between 1992 and 1996. African
Americans, who constitute 29 percent of the city's population,
filed 53 percent of the complaints in 1996. In San Diego, in contrast, complaints filed against the police fell modestly during
this period.

Law professor Herman Goldstein of the University of Wisconsin, regarded as one of the intellectual founders of problem-
oriented policing, cautions us to recall that in evaluating
policing today, "the bottom line is not crime, the bottom line is
the racial tensions in our large urban areas, and there's no escaping that. We may, in fact, have an impact upon crime, disorder,
and fear, but if in the course of doing that, we substantially increase tensions in the community, we've made matters worse.[19]

NOTES

1. The discussion in this section examines the relationship between imprisonment and the crime rate as measured by the FBI's Uniform Crime Reports, commonly referred to as "the crime rate." Victimization studies by the Justice Department offer a somewhat different measure of these issues. We use the FBI data here because they are the figures generally cited in public discussions of crime, and because they are weighted toward the more serious crimes that are likely to lead to a prison term upon conviction.

2. James Alan Fox, "Trends in Juvenile Violence," Department of Justice, March 1996, pp. 4–5.

3. Melissa Sickmund, Howard N. Snyder, and Eileen Poe-Yamagata, *Juvenile Offenders and Victims: 1997 Update on Violence*, National Center for Juvenile Justice, June 1997, p. 13.

4. Elliott Currie, *Crime and Punishment in America* (New York: Metropolitan Books, 1998), p. 26.

5. Ibid., pp. 25–26.

6. Albert J. Reiss, Jr. and Jeffrey A. Roth, eds., *Understanding and Preventing Violence* (Washington, D.C.: National Academy Press, 1993), p. 6.

7. Christopher Nuttall, "What Works in Dealing with Crime?: An International Perspective," in *International Comparisons in Criminal Justice* (London: National Association for the Care and Resettlement of Offenders, 1995), p. 10.

8. Franklin E. Zimring and Gordon Hawkins, *Incapacitation*, (New York: Oxford University Press, 1995), p. 126.

9. Michael K. Block, *Supply Side Imprisonment Policy* (Washington, D.C.: National Institute of Justice, July 1997).

10. Ibid., p. 12.

11. William C. Collins, "A History of Recent Corrections Is a History of Court Involvement," *Corrections Today* (Aug. 1995), p. 114.

12. Jean Johnson, "Americans' Views on Crime and Law Enforcement," *National Institute of Justice Journal* (Sept. 1997), p. 10.

13. Jonathan P. Caulkins, et al., *Mandatory Minimum Drug Sentences: Throwing Away the Key or the Taxpayers' Money?* (Santa Monica, Calif.: RAND Corporation, 1997).

14. William Glaberson, "Crime in New York Area Falls, but Some Pockets Defy Trends, *The New York Times*, Feb. 27, 1997, p. A26.

15. Paul Goldstein et al., "Crack and homicide in New York City: A conceptually-based event analysis," *Contemporary Drug Problems* 16 (1989), pp. 651–87.

16. Andrew Lang Golub and Bruce D. Johnson, *Crack's Decline: Some Surprises Across U.S. Cities*, (Washington, D.C.: National Institute of Justice, July 1997), p. 6.

17. Ibid., p. 11.

18. Judith A. Greene, "Zero Tolerance: A Case Study of Police Policies and Practices in New York City," Institute on Criminal Justice, University of Minnesota Law School, May 1998.

19. Thomas V. Brady, *Measuring What Matters* (Washington, D.C.: National Institute of Justice, December 1996), p. 9.

6—The Limits of the Criminal Justice System on Crime Control

Our reliance on the criminal justice system as our primary crime control mechanism has blinded us to the complexity of crime and ways to control it, and has thus encouraged heightened expectations about the role of courts and prisons in providing public safety. Since by definition these institutions are reactive systems that come into play *after* a crime has been committed, it should hardly be surprising that their role in controlling crime will always be limited. While most of us recognize intuitively that families, communities, and other institutions necessarily play a major role in the socialization process, political demagoguery has promoted the centrality of the criminal justice system as the means by which communities can be made safer.

Why have the policies adopted in recent years have been so ineffective and arguably, even counterproductive, in addressing the problem of crime? Several factors in particular stand out.

THE CRIMINAL JUSTICE SYSTEM "FUNNEL" MISSES MOST CRIMES

Many Americans have had the experience of calling 911 to report an ongoing or just-completed crime. At that point, the police are notified that a crime has been committed and, depending on the seriousness of the offense and the availability of police resources, they may or may not begin an investigation or take some other action.

But most crimes, even serious crimes, do not even result in a call to 911, let alone an arrest or conviction. The "reactive" character of the criminal justice system—not an "ineffective" police force or "soft" judges—is what limits the utility of courts and prisons for crime control purposes.

Criminologists sometimes describe the dynamics of the system as resembling a funnel. At the top of the funnel are all the personal and household crimes committed in a given year, which totaled 42.4 million in 1994, according to national victimization estimates.[1] ("Victimless" crimes such as drug transactions are not included in these surveys, nor are commercial burglaries or thefts.) We know of many of these crimes only because of surveys asking people if they have been a victim of crime in the preceding twelve months, regardless of whether they reported this crime to the police.

The rate at which victims *don't* report crimes to the police is, in fact, quite remarkable: this is the first dropoff in the criminal justice funnel. Nationally, only about a third of all crimes are actually reported; even for serious violent crimes, the reporting rate is only about 50 percent. What explains this large dropoff?

First, many victims don't report crimes because they don't believe the police can do anything. For example, a bike is stolen from a schoolyard or a garage that was left open. Realistically, it is unlikely that police departments with stretched resources will be able to devote much attention to such crimes or have much success in apprehending an offender.

But crimes that are more serious than bike theft also result in substantial proportions of nonreporting. Only just over a third of victims of rape and sexual assault, for example, report these offenses to the police. This results from a combination of factors involving the victim-offender relationship, a lack of confidence in the police, and degree of harm suffered. Until relatively recently, many women often felt doubly victimized by sexual assaults, first by the perpetrator and second by the insensitivity of criminal justice personnel. Many police departments now employ special units, staffed largely by female officers, to hear these complaints and to aid victims in obtaining counseling and other services. This has had the ironic impact of making it nearly impossible to interpret increases in reports of sex offenses in the past two decades; it is not clear whether more women are being raped and sexually assaulted or whether victims are more likely to report such offenses.

Other violent crimes that never come to the attention of the police may involve assaults among rival drug dealers or people who have a criminal record. In these cases, neither victim nor offender may want the police to get involved—so the incident goes undetected in official statistics.

Finally, many crimes are of a less serious nature than one might imagine from reading news reports of crime victim surveys. For example, more than half of all assaults involve attempts without a weapon and result in no injury. Likewise, seven out of ten robberies result in no injury. These may be frightening, to be sure, but they are clearly on a different order of magnitude than other violent crimes.

While it has long been assumed that crime-reporting is less common in minority communities, this does not in fact appear to currently be the case. Data from the Bureau of Justice Statistics indicate that, from 1973 to the present, crime-reporting rates for both violent offenses and personal thefts have been somewhat higher for blacks than whites. This is not the result, however, of greater black confidence or trust in the police. Of the persons who did *not* report crimes to the police, 16.6 percent of blacks stated that they believed the police would not want to be bothered, or would be ineffective or biased, compared to 9.2 percent of whites.[2]

One reason for the higher rate of black reporting appears to be related to the harm involved in the offense. Twenty percent of whites who did not report crimes stated their reason as being that the object was recovered or the offender was unsuccessful, compared to 12.4 percent of blacks. It is also conceivable that whites may have greater access to other means of coping with the consequences of their victimization, thereby reducing their need to call upon the police. For example, low-income people of all races are more likely to call the police even for noncrime difficulties, such as family problems or medical emergencies.[3]

For a complex set of reasons, then, nearly two thirds of all serious crimes never even come to the attention of the police and, obviously, can never be "solved." (The primary exception in this regard relates to auto theft, which has a 90 percent reporting rate. However, this reflects the reporting requirements imposed on car owners in order to file insurance claims.) It is also unlikely that these proportions can be increased to any significant extent. For property crimes, absent some remarkable shift in the number of personnel or the number of crimes, the police will never be able to solve many of these offenses and, therefore, there will continue to be little incentive to report them. While assaultive crimes are reported to a somewhat greater extent, for the reasons described above it is also unlikely that any substantial increases will occur. Despite changes in police technology and other factors, reporting rates only rose modestly between 1973 and 1990, from 32.4 percent to 37.7 percent.[4]

Nevertheless, a little over a third of crimes are reported to the police. What happens to them? The criminal justice funnel continues to reduce the number of cases handled by the system—only about one fifth even result in a suspect being arrested and charged with an offense. Here, too, the problem is not primarily one of lazy or inefficient police (although improvements in policing can have an impact in this area), but rather the dynamics of crime itself.

Consider the difference between bank robbery and burglary, for example. Bank robberies are far more likely to lead to a suspect's arrest for several reasons. First, they are serious offenses, both in their potential for violence and due to the fact that they threaten the viability of a significant institution in society. Both federal and state laws may be violated in a bank robbery, and so police agencies at different levels of government may be brought in to work on a case. Security considerations have led to virtually all banks now being equipped with video cameras, so that in addition to witnesses being present, perpetrators are often caught on camera—which is extremely unusual for most crimes and immeasurably beneficial to the police.

In the case of burglary, though, no such advantages accrue to law enforcement. The crime is only of local, not federal, concern; there are generally no witnesses to the crime; and rarely is there such clear evidence of the offender's identity as a videotape.

At this point in the system, then, only about one in thirteen offenses, whether reported or not, has even led to an arrest. But the funnel effect still continues to reduce the scope of the system's impact.

First, not all arrests lead to prosecution. After examining the evidence, particularly the strength of the case against the accused, prosecutors frequently decide to drop charges or to charge the crime as a lesser offense. While police may make an arrest because they believe they have "probable cause" to do so, prosecutors who have to prove a case in court "beyond a reasonable doubt" may not have sufficient evidence. For example, the main witness to an offense may be a rival drug dealer or someone with a long criminal history whose veracity may be challenged in court.

Although the notorious O. J. Simpson criminal case was atypical in many respects, the quality of its evidence was in some ways fairly usual. A double murder was committed in which there was some circumstantial evidence pointing to the possibility that Simpson was the killer—the bloody glove, a history of spousal abuse, Simpson's hand injury, and other factors. But, like so many cases, the evidence was less convincing than many a prosecutor (or jury) would like. There were no eyewitnesses to the crime, no videotapes, and no murder weapon found.

Finally, prosecutors will often make use of the discretion available to them to sort out the more serious cases from those involving less harm, just as victims do. Among assault cases, for example, about one half of aggravated assaults are reported to the police, whereas only about one third of simple assaults are reported. This most likely reflects victims' perceptions of the degree of harm they have suffered. Given the realities of an overburdened criminal justice system, prosecutors may also appropriately give greater priority to the more serious cases, on the belief that these offenders may represent a greater threat to public safety.

Of the cases that are brought to trial or, more commonly, lead to a plea agreement, a substantial proportion of guilty verdicts are obtained (although some cases that begin as felonies ultimately result in misdemeanor convictions). When a felony conviction is obtained, though, the likelihood of incarceration is quite high. Bureau of Justice Statistics figures for 1994 indicate that seven out of ten convicted state felons were sentenced to incarceration—45 percent received a prison sentence and 26 percent a jail term (although this may include time spent in jail awaiting trial). Not surprisingly, the more serious the felony, the greater likelihood of incarceration. For violent offenses, 82 percent of offenders received either a prison or jail term.

Figure 6-1 displays the overall operation of the criminal justice funnel for serious violent crimes committed in 1994. We use violent crimes here, as opposed to all crimes, because these should presumably show the criminal justice system at its most efficient: these crimes are more likely to be reported to the police, to receive police attention, and to result in a sentence of incarceration upon conviction. There were about 3.9 million victimizations for violent offenses in 1994 for rape, robbery, aggravated assault, and homicide (which is included here even though, for obvious reasons, it does not show up in surveys of victims). Just under half of these, 1.9 million, were reported to the police, and of these, about 41 percent, or 779,000, resulted in an arrest. Only 143,000 of the arrests, or about 18 percent, resulted in a felony conviction, though. Some of these arrests resulted in misdemeanor convictions, some were referred to and disposed of in juvenile court, and others were dismissed or found not guilty for lack of evidence. Of those who were convicted of a violent felony, 82 percent were sentenced to a period of incarceration. These 117,000 sentences represented just 3 percent of all the serious violent offenses originally committed. Even if the system could somehow manage to double or triple these rates, the overall impact is obviously limited.

Figure 6-1

The Criminal Justice "Funnel"

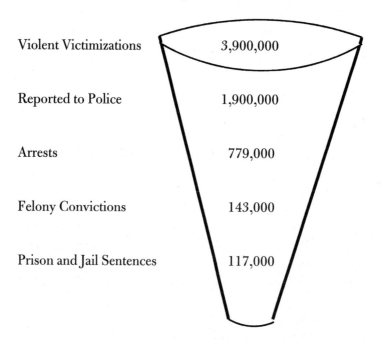

Violent Victimizations	3,900,000
Reported to Police	1,900,000
Arrests	779,000
Felony Convictions	143,000
Prison and Jail Sentences	117,000

Sources: Bureau of Justice Statistics, Criminal Victimization in the United States, 1994; "Felony Sentences in State Courts, 1994"; FBI, Uniform Crime Reports, 1994

Even if we isolate the most serious offense, homicide, we observe the same dynamics: a *Los Angeles Times* analysis of more than 9,000 homicides committed over a five-year period found that only one in three resulted in a conviction, due to limited police resources, weak evidence, and the large volume of crime.[5]

We should note as well that the dynamics of the criminal justice funnel are not unique to the U.S. system. In England, for example, only about 3 percent of offenses result in a conviction.[6]

This is not to say, of course, that the overwhelming number of crimes being committed makes incarceration of offenders completely inconsequential. The winnowing effect of the criminal justice funnel is somewhat offset by the fact that while the number of cases resulting in conviction or incarceration is very low, the number of *crimes* resolved through the system is actually somewhat higher. A burglar, for example, may break into five homes but only be caught and convicted for one of them. If the burglar is then locked up for the one conviction, essentially all five crimes have been resolved. (The victims, of course, would have preferred to know that the offender who had burglarized their home had been convicted, but for crime control purposes, the offense has been resolved.)

Locking up an individual offender may have some impact on the individual. As an overall strategy, though, the reactive nature of the system suggests that attempting to control crime primarily through incarceration is a myopic approach. The recognition of this dynamic has been a primary impetus for the development of community policing that emphasizes a problem-solving approach to conflict rather than just making arrests.

DIMINISHING RETURNS

A second critical factor that limits the utility of imprisonment as a means of controlling crime emerges from a close examination of the continuing increases in the institutional population over the past quarter century. Essentially, as the prison population has escalated, the offenders who are locked up are ever-less serious offenders on average than in previous years. The result: diminishing returns in crime control.

In order to understand this, consider the workings of any court system. A state legislature trying to "toughen" its sentencing policies can accomplish the goal in one of two ways. As noted in Chapter 2, either a greater proportion of convicted offenders can be sentenced to prison or those who are sentenced to prison can be required to stay longer. If the latter strategy is undertaken, the legislature will run up against the limitations imposed by the demographics of crime: crime rates tend to diminish with age, resulting in diminishing returns for a longer-sentence strategy. (We will return to this issue later.) The option of choosing to send a greater number of offenders to prison, though, has its own set of diminishing returns, too.

If a choice is made to increase the number of offenders receiving a prison term, relatively few additional violent offenders who are not already receiving a prison term will be sentenced to one. At the same time, considerably greater numbers of nonviolent property and drug offenders will be brought in. Though the public generally places a priority on using prison cells for violent offenders, a policy to imprison more offenders would likely have the opposite impact: greater numbers of nonviolent offenders would be locked up.

The reasons why greater numbers of less serious offenders are locked up over time is clearest in the realm of drug offenses. The typical drug ring consists of a handful of "kingpins" at the top of the distribution network, a modest number of wholesalers in the mid-levels, and large numbers of street-level sellers. On those relatively rare occasions when kingpins are apprehended, they are virtually always sentenced to harsh prison terms, as are most of the wholesalers. So by insisting on a dramatic increase in the number of drug offenders in prison, as states have since 1980, they ensure that the vast majority of new prisoners will be lower-level offenders.

As we saw in Chapter 2, a substantial portion of the rise in the inmate population for the decade 1985–95 consisted of drug offenders—35 percent at the state level and 74 percent at the federal level. This increase has been disproportionately felt by African Americans: 42 percent of the prison population increase from 1985 to 1995 among blacks nationally consisted of drug offenders.[7]

Looking at California, a state that quadrupled its prison

population in the decade 1980–90, we see similar dynamics. While 60 percent of state prison inmates in 1980 had been committed to prison for a violent offense, only 27 percent of the additional prison space added in the following ten years was used to incarcerate violent offenders.[8]

The phenomenon of diminishing returns has a substantial impact on the value of prison as a crime control tool. In Chapter 4, we saw the statistical miscalculations that can result from assumptions of the "average" number of crimes avoided through incarceration. However, research by several prominent academics has now provided a corrective with estimates of the impact of diminishing returns.

These criminologists have developed statistical models to compare offending rates between imprisoned offenders and those offenders who are not caught.[9] Inmate surveys conducted by the RAND Corporation in three states in the 1980s have provided criminologists with a baseline estimate of the frequency of offending among those imprisoned. Those studies concluded that some of the imprisoned robbers and burglars reported committing well over one hundred crimes a year, even though the median rate was considerably less. However, offenders who are locked up are likely to be frequent offenders: a burglar who commits 100 burglaries a year is both more likely to be apprehended and more likely to be sentenced to prison than a burglar who commits 5 crimes a year. This data has led some proponents of increased incarceration to overstate the potential benefits of incarceration, based on the assumption that each succeeding offender would commit crimes at the same rate as the average inmate in prison. Yet, recent research shows that, among robbers and burglars, offenders who are not arrested and remain free commit an average of 1–3 robberies and 2–4 burglaries a year, whereas incarcerated offenders had committed these crimes at a rate 10–50 times higher. These findings do not tell us, of course, whether any individual offender should be sentenced to prison or not. That determination will reflect an assessment of the seriousness of the offense, the threat to the community, and the range of sentencing options available.

In terms of overall public policy, the dynamics of diminishing returns suggest that the expansion of the prison system tends increasingly to respond to lower-level criminal activity on average. Given that incarcerating an offender costs about $20,000 annually, policymakers need to analyze the various levels and forms of impact on crime control that could be achieved by applying this spending to either alternative criminal justice or community-based interventions.

The limitations imposed by these diminishing returns have been summarized in a comprehensive National Institute of Justice study on crime prevention prepared for Congress: "It is clear that the most serious offenders such as serial rapists should be incapacitated. However, locking up those who are *not* high-rate, serious offenders or those who are at the end of their criminal careers is extremely expensive."[10]

Even James Q. Wilson, considered one of the leading conservative scholars in the field of criminal justice, has agreed that, due to the phenomenon of diminishing returns and the difficulty of increasing deterrence, "very large increases in the prison population can produce only modest reductions in crime rates."[11]

DEMOGRAPHICS

The limitations of the criminal justice system as a means of crime control are further revealed by assessing the demographics of crime commission, particularly the fact that young males in the 15–24 age group commit a disproportionate amount of crime. In 1995, for example, 38 percent of arrests nationally were of persons in this range. For whatever combination of reasons, this factor holds true across class lines and generally across national boundaries.

The demographics of crime commission can be seen in Figure 6-2. As we can see, the offense rates for robbery and burglary peak at age 17, and for aggravated assault at 18. But note also the fairly steep decline in these rates within just a few years of 18. Thus, by the age of 21, the rates at which persons are committing robbery and burglary falls to half, while the aggravated assault rate reaches this level by the mid-30s. As we shall see in detail later, much of this is due to the maturing of youth and the assumption of adult responsibilities — stable relationships, education, and employment.

Now, contrast this with the profile of offenders in prison. The average inmate in a state prison as of 1991 was 30 years old. Thus, Figure 6-2 indicates that, as a group, these individuals are on the "downside" of their "criminal careers." This is not to suggest that a 30-year-old Charles Manson or Son of Sam is past being a threat to public safety; but from the point of view of investing tax dollars and controlling crime, each succeeding year of incarceration for a more typical offender is "buying" less crime control.

Thus, we see the folly in particular of policies such as "three strikes and you're out" which require sentences of life without parole. Leaving aside the difficult question of how much punishment is "enough" to satisfy the demands of justice, it nevertheless is clear that there are diminishing returns for public safety the longer an offender remains in prison.

Why, though, would such an apparently irrational system evolve, one that locks up offenders well after their peak crime-committing years? Much of the discrepancy between the high-crime years and the older ages of inmates results from the dynamics of sentencing practices. Usually, first-time offenders are incarcerated only for a serious crime; thus, for a first-time property offense or even a minor assault, an offender is likely to be placed on probation, be required to pay a fine or other obligation, and generally see relatively little of the inside of a jail or prison cell. (This is less and less true for drug offenses: mandatory minimum sentences often require harsh prison terms even for first offenses.) If the offender continues to engage in crime,

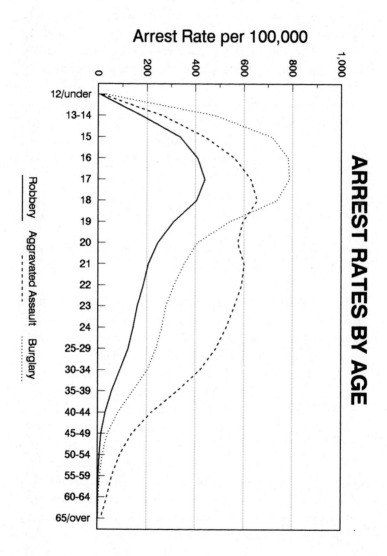

Figure 6-2
Arrest Rates by Age

the consequences generally escalate, resulting in jail or prison terms by the second or third offense.

The result is a conflict between competing goals of sentencing. For the goal of incapacitating offenders to reduce crime, there are questionable benefits to be derived from escalating sentences, particularly given the high cost of imprisonment; however, if the goal is punishment, prison is clearly one means of achieving that, albeit an expensive method in many regards. As we shall see later, incarceration has deleterious effects on an individual's earning potential and results in the absence of a potential contributing member of a family and community. The question then becomes whether sentencing options other than incarceration can meet the punitive goals of the system in a way that is either more cost-effective or has fewer negative consequences for the individual and society.*

A qualification of the demographic chart above is that the age–crime data refer to the population as a whole. A 30-year-old inmate with a history of criminal activity is presumably more likely to engage in future crimes than is a 30-year-old with no history of offending. Nevertheless, while the absolute level of criminal activity may be higher for those with a record, here, too, the declining effects over time and with age remain the same. For example, a Justice Department survey of recidivism rates conducted in the 1980s found that rearrest rates for offenders released from prison who were 45 years of age or older were 41 percent lower than for offenders in the 18–24 age bracket.[12]

Some might argue that since crime rates spike so rapidly in the late teen years, that we should incarcerate many more of those offenders. Aside from the huge cost involved in such a policy and the likely negative consequences on life opportuni-

*Note also that many observers are increasingly questioning the value of the punitive orientation of the sentencing system itself, both from a moral and a crime control standpoint. Our point here is merely to suggest that as long as punishment remains a central focus of most court systems, responses other than imprisonment will often be more practical and reasonable.

ties this would entail, it is also certain that such an approach would be far from efficient from a cost perspective. Since such a large fraction of the young offending population already ceases its criminal activities within a few years, any massive increase in the use of imprisonment would only result in overkill. Further, criminologists have never been able to predict with any more certainty than the flip of a coin which of these offenders will continue to be involved in crime over a long period of time. Thus, for every offender who might be "selectively incapacitated," as has sometimes been proposed, another who would not have been engaged in future crime would be locked up. Not only should this offend our sense of justice, but it would not prove to be particularly wise as a crime reducing strategy.

THE "REPLACEMENT" EFFECT

A basic tenet of incarceration as a crime control method is that incapacitated offenders are unable to commit any crimes. Thus, the increase in the number of state and federal prisoners from 196,000 to 1,159,000 from 1972 to 1997 on the surface should have had a significant impact on crime rates merely due to this phenomenon. As we have seen, though, little of this occurred.

A primary explanation for this phenomenon holds that some offenders are "replaced" on the streets by others ready to take their place. As a result, imprisoning an offender will not always reduce crime.

Consider two offenders, one a serial rapist, the other a street-level drug seller. When the rapist is convicted and incarcerated, a certain amount of public safety has been achieved; however, there is no "market" for rapists in a neighborhood—individuals either engage in this behavior or do not.

With the drug seller, though, a thriving market exists with the potential for lucrative profits (although these are attained less often than in popular mythology or in the minds of young drug dealers). Thus, when the drug seller is locked up, a job opening has been created on that street corner. With few references or resources required to obtain this position, in far too many urban neighborhoods the opening is filled virtually within minutes of the previous seller's arrest.

This phenomenon was illustrated in a 1996 report of the Wisconsin Governor's Task Force on Sentencing and Corrections.[13] Members of the Task Force described hearing police testimony regarding a street corner in Milwaukee at which 94 drug arrests were made over a three-month period. Despite this, the police and community reported that following the arrests the corner still remained a trouble spot and a center of drug activity.

People of good will may debate whether drug sellers, even low-level ones, should be incarcerated and whether that somehow conveys a "message" to the community. This should not be confused, though, with deceiving ourselves into believing that any serious impact has been made on the drug trade itself.

We are still left with the question, though, of why there are so many potential offenders available to "replace" those who are apprehended by the justice system. Remember that despite a doubling of the prison population in the 1980s, crime rates failed to decline during this time — so either there was a greater propensity to commit crime among the population in the free world or a greater number of crimes were committed by each offender. An economic analysis of this issue in the context of the impact of labor market opportunities as they pertained to crime rates in the 1980s and 1990s found that declining job opportunities for young urban males, along with changes in wages for legitimate work and measures of inequality, increased the propensity to commit crime among those in the free world.[14] The author concluded that "although research has not yielded sufficiently strong results to predict reliably how much crime might fall if the job market for crime-prone groups improved substantively, the limited estimates we have are consistent with an expectation that such effects would not be negligible."[15]

LOST OPPORTUNITIES

Our discussion of the limitations of the criminal justice system as a mechanism for crime control, while necessary, risks obscuring some fundamental issues. The most significant is that, regardless of whether one believes that imprisonment is "effective" in controlling crime, it is hardly the only option by which a society can respond to problem behaviors. All nations maintain prison systems, but the degree to which these are used as a primary determinant of crime policy varies broadly.

Thus, even if one were to conclude that prison is cost-effective—that the value of crime prevented is greater than the cost of incarceration—this does not mean that other social policy interventions might not be equally or even more effective. In fact, a good deal of research has documented such findings, showing that drug treatment is more effective than mandatory sentences,[16] and that interventions with high risk families are more beneficial than three strikes policies.[17] Given limited resources in a society, the choice is how those resources can be most effectively utilized.

The other risk entailed in an analysis that involves measures of cost-effectiveness is that one can lose sight of the human factors involved. When one of our loved ones is ill or in trouble, most of us rarely hesitate to employ whatever financial and human resources we can muster to deal with the problem. This might involve specialized medical care, tutors for learning-disabled children, or a nursing home for an ageing relative. Deciding how to use taxpayer funds wisely is a contentious issue, of course. One is led to wonder, however, to what extent the zeal with which efforts are made to demonstrate the value of imprisonment is a reflection of the "otherness" of those being imprisoned.

NOTES

1. Bureau of Justice Statistics, *Criminal Victimization in the United States, 1994* (Washington, D.C.: Bureau of Justice Statistics, May 1997), p. 6.
2. Ibid., p. 96.

3. Samuel Walker, Cassia Spohn, and Miriam DeLone, *The Color of Justice* (Belmont, Calif.: Wadsworth, 1996), p. 90.

4. Bureau of Justice Statistics, *Criminal Victimization in the United States: 1973–90 Trends* (Washington, D.C.: Bureau of Justice Statistics, December 1992), p. 123.

5. Fredric N. Tulsky and Ted Rohrlich, "Only 1 in 3 Killings in County is Punished," *Los Angeles Times*, Dec. 1, 1996, p. A1.

6. Roger Graef, "Crime, Justice and the Media," in *International Comparisons in Criminal Justice* (London: National Association for the Care and Resettlement of Offenders, 1995), p. 24.

7. Christopher J. Mumola and Allen J. Beck, *Prisoners in 1996* (Washington, D.C.: Bureau of Justice Statistics, June 1997), p. 10.

8. Franklin E. Zimring and Gordon Hawkins, *Crime Is Not the Problem: Lethal Violence in America* (New York: Oxford University Press, 1997), p. 18.

9. Jose A. Canela-Cacho, Alfred Blumstein, and Jacqueline Cohen, "Relationship Between the Offending Frequency of Imprisoned and Free Offenders," *Criminology 35* (Feb. 1997).

10. Doris Layton MacKenzie, "Criminal Justice and Crime Prevention," in Lawrence W. Sherman, et al., *Preventing Crime: What Works, What Doesn't, What's Promising* (Washington, D.C.: National Institute of Justice, 1997), pp. 9–51.

11. James Q. Wilson, "Crime and Public Policy," in James Q. Wilson and Joan Petersilia, eds., *Crime* (San Francisco: Institute for Contemporary Studies, 1995), p. 501.

12. Allen Beck and Bernard Shipley, *Recidivism of Prisoners Released in 1983* (Washington, D.C.: Bureau of Justice Statistics, April 1989).

13. Governor's Task Force on Sentencing and Corrections, *Final Report*, Dec. 17, 1996, p. 3.

14. Richard B. Freeman, "The Labor Market," in Wilson and Petersilia, *Crime*, pp. 171–91.

15. Ibid., p. 191.

16. Jonathan P. Caulkins, et al., *Mandatory Minimum Drug Sentences* (Santa Monica, Calif.: RAND Corporation, 1997).

17. Peter W. Greenwood, et al., *Diverting Children from a Life of Crime* (Santa Monica, Calif.: RAND Corporation, 1996).

7—African Americans and the Criminal Justice System

I wonder if because it is blacks getting shot down, because it is blacks who are going to jail in massive numbers, whether we—the total we, black and white—care as much? If we started to put white America in jail at the same rate that we're putting black America in jail, I wonder whether our collective feelings would be the same, or would we be putting pressure on the president and our elected officials not to lock up America, but to save America?

— Former Atlanta Police Chief Eldrin Bell[1]

Imagine that you are a pregnant mother at your first meeting of a childbirth class in Harlem or the east side of Detroit or South Central Los Angeles. All ten members of the class are African American women who, coincidentally, are expecting boys. After a general overview regarding what to expect of pregnancy and childbirth, the teacher tells you all that she also has some news regarding the future of your children—three out of ten of your boys will spend time in prison. While she can't predict which of your boys will be the three, national statistics suggest that this is how their lives will turn out.

This is a rather bleak scenario, of course, and one that is not generally incorporated into childbirth classes—but it is accurate nonetheless. Police Chief Bell's question is quite apt; would Americans permit these circumstances to continue if the odds were three in ten for boys from other racial and ethnic groups? The answer should be obvious.

At the close of the twentieth century, race, crime, and the criminal justice system are inextricably linked. A walk through nearly any courtroom or prison in the United States reveals a sea of black and brown faces at the defendant's table and in the prison yard. Half of all prison inmates are now African American, and another 17 percent are Hispanic—percentages *far* out of proportion to their numbers in the general population.*

Although we have become so inured to these gross disparities that they seem almost inevitable, in point of fact they mirror other historical trends. As European immigrant groups swept into the United States at the turn of the century, their involvement in crime and the criminal justice system was disproportionate to their numbers in the population. Many of the same fears voiced today about African Americans were raised then about the immigrants; writings of the time reveal that the connection between immigration and crime had nearly become a "national obsession." For example, a 1911 study by the United States Immigration Commission described various races and nationalities as "exhibiting clearly defined criminal characteristics." Italians were depicted as being prominently involved in crimes of violence, the Irish in drunkenness and vagrancy, and Jews in prostitution and crimes against property.[2]

This is not to suggest that the criminal justice system and African Americans have not been linked throughout American history. Following the end of slavery in the South, for instance, white planters, businessmen, and politicians devised new ways to keep the black population subservient and exploited. Historian David Oshinsky describes how the new methods being devised flowed out of the longstanding racist mindset: "Southern whites had long viewed criminal behavior as natural to the Negro. They took his stealing for granted, as a biological flaw."[3]

Once slaves were freed, they had the "opportunity" to commit crimes beyond the confines of the slave plantation. As more blacks were arrested for crimes, the proportion of blacks among the inmate population soared, as did the number of inmates overall. In a region where many of the prisons had been dam-

---

*Much of the discussion in this and the following two chapters focuses on African Americans and the criminal justice system. Many of the dynamics in this regard may apply to Hispanics as well, but unfortunately state and federal government surveys are often incomplete or inconsistent in providing data on Hispanics.

aged or destroyed during the war, this created substantial strains on prison systems that had nowhere to house the expanding inmate population. The ingenious solution was the convict leasing system, in which the state contracted with local businessmen and farmers to use the labor of inmates in exchange for providing them with food and housing. In Mississippi, the state initially paid the contractor for taking the prisoners off its hands; later, contractors had to pay a fee for use of the labor.

Compared to slavery, the new system had many economic advantages for the employers:

> [The leasing of convict labor] plugged the major weakness of the old system: the high fixed cost of labor. Under the sublease, an employer was not stuck with a set number of prisoners over a long period of time. He did not have to feed, clothe, and guard them when there was little work to be done. He could now lease convicts according to his specific, or seasonal, needs.[4]

From the laborer's point of view, of course, the system was extremely brutal. Oshinsky reports that the annual mortality rate for the convict population in Mississippi in the 1880s ranged from 9 to 16 percent. The black rate was much higher than the white rate; 126 blacks out of 735 inmates died in 1882, compared to 2 out of 83 whites.[5]

Even with this phenomenon as background, however, by the early twentieth century prison admission records show a very different picture from what we see today. Although we have no firm data on prison admissions for the first quarter of this century, records have been kept consistently since 1926. They indicate that African Americans made up a smaller proportion of those sentenced to prison during the early part of this century than is now the case. Black offenders represented 21 percent of those admitted to prison in 1926, compared to half of all prison admissions today.[6] How can we account for this rather striking anomaly?

Part of the explanation may lie in the nature of the societal response to crime, of which the formal criminal justice system is only one aspect. Due to patterns of residential segregation, most crime is intraracial. For the most part, people get into fights with their neighbors, break into homes in their communities, and commit sexual assaults against people they know in some capacity. If blacks and whites largely live apart from each other—often in patterns that are more entrenched than a century ago—most offenders will therefore victimize someone of the same race.

Historically, as long as black crime was concentrated within black communities, it was generally of little concern to law enforcement. Blacks were essentially unrepresented among law enforcement officials and political leadership, and so there was little sensitivity or interest in devoting resources to communities viewed as second-class.

When black crime spilled over into white communities, though, or at least was perceived to, the heavy hand of justice was employed to its full extent. Often this had little to do with the formal mechanisms of the justice system, as the several thousand lynchings of the early decades of the twentieth century attest. The racist use of the death penalty worked to similar ends: prior to being declared unconstitutional in modern times, use of the death penalty for the crime of rape was a relatively frequent occurrence. Of the 455 persons executed for rape in the first half of this century, 405, or almost 90 percent, were black men. Looking at the race of rape victims, it has been reported that "no cases are known in which any white man was executed for the rape of a black woman."[7]

By the time of the *Brown v. Board of Education* decision of 1954, African Americans constituted about 30 percent of those persons admitted to state and federal prisons. This figure should have been disturbing, since it was substantially higher than the African American share of the national population. But by 1988 this proportion had increased still more dramatically, to the point where blacks represented *half* of all prison admissions.

Considering the times, this could be viewed as a rather strange development. For a period of thirty years following 1954, the nation experienced the civil rights movement and the opening of significant (if still limited) economic and political opportunities for African Americans and other historically disadvantaged groups. Within the criminal justice system, blacks rose through the ranks to become police chiefs, judges, and prison officials — not in proportion to their share of the population, to be sure, but certainly to a greater degree than in the days of all-white justice. Since many of the legal obstacles to full participation in society had been removed, and at least some African Americans had been able to take advantage of leadership opportunities opening up in various fields, the proportion of blacks locked up in the nation's prisons should not have risen.

The reason for the rise rests in the demographic changes taking place in the post–World War II period, and the central role of African Americans in many of those changes. With the massive closings of the Appalachian coal mines due to the end of steam-driven railway locomotion and the rapid expansion of highly mechanized strip-mining in other parts of the country, whites moved north into the auto and steel plants of Detroit and Youngstown. At the same time, with the mechanization of cotton agriculture, large numbers of blacks moved from the Deep South to northern factory jobs and to the urban ghettoes of New York, Chicago, and many other cities.

This was accompanied almost simultaneously by the emergence of the "baby boom" generation. The return of soldiers from the war, along with the growing economy, had fueled a dramatic increase in family expansion. By the 1960s, this new generation was making a much younger United States.

All was not necessarily well with the new face of the country, though. Blacks who were newly arrived from the South found patterns of segregation and discrimination different in form from those they had left behind, but no less pernicious in many regards. Housing patterns in urban areas were often as segregated in the North as they were in the rural South. This phenomenon was partly a result of the poverty of the new arrivals, but it was largely a result of real-estate decisions by banks, insurance companies, and property brokers which effectively divided cities along racial lines. Interchange between the races was often even more restricted than in the South, where at least there was extensive contact within communities, albeit in caste roles. In the more urbanized North, though, many whites could go about their daily business with virtually no interaction with blacks, aside from possibly sitting next to a 'Negro' on a bus or train.

Northern law enforcement officials were often as unresponsive to crime in the black community as their counterparts were in the South. On those occasions when they did respond, their faces were generally white, representing the Irish and other ethnic groups that had long used the police force as a means of occupational advancement.

Most important, while overall unemployment rates were declining in the 1960s, rates of unemployment for nonwhite youth were increasing—as was the proportion of nonwhites not even looking for work. Thus, the official unemployment rate for nonwhite males aged 18–19 rose from 10 percent in 1952 to 20 percent in 1967, while the proportion of nonwhite youth either working or looking for work declined from 80 percent in 1952 to 63 percent by 1967.[8]

These labor market changes alone were sufficient to explain increasing crime rates for youths in the 1960s. Essentially, those young people who are so isolated from the mainstream that they are not even looking for work have little incentive to conform to societal norms, since they do not perceive themselves as having an opportunity to share in the rewards of the working world.

Even among those youth who are engaged in the labor market, but largely confined to low-wage jobs, the phenomenon of "relative deprivation" became a contributing factor to crime.[9] It was and is not just a question of whether one has enough to eat and survive, but how one's material standards compare to others' and to perceptions regarding whether hard work results in appropriate rewards. For example, wealthy people who commit economic crimes clearly are not lacking material rewards, but may view themselves almost in competition with others who are even wealthier.

A GENERATION BEHIND BARS

By the 1980s, we witnessed the remarkable result of some of the positive changes set in motion during the 1960s: The ranks of the black middle class expanded during these years and, while racism hardly disappeared, substantial numbers of African American families began populating suburban areas and sending their children on to secondary and postsecondary education.

But for those left behind in inner cities life had become a cruel parody of what the civil rights movement had promised. Rather than finding new vistas and opportunities, inner city residents inhabited a place isolated from the social and economic changes going on in the wider world. As stock speculators and others reaped huge profits from the emerging globalized economy, the domestic divide between haves and have-nots only worsened. And, increasingly the clutches of the nation's prisons and jails became the temporary or permanent home of the local downtrodden.

By the mid-1990s, the number of African Americans within the criminal justice system had reached unprecedented levels. Half of the inmates in the nation's prisons were African American, compared to their 13 percent share of the population, and one in fourteen adult black males was locked up in a prison or jail on any given day.

For young black men, the situation was far worse. A study by The Sentencing Project found that in 1989 nearly one in four black males in the age group 20–29 was under some form of criminal justice supervision on any given day—either in prison or jail, or on probation or parole. A follow-up study in 1995 then found that this figure had increased to almost one in three, a remarkable rise over a short period of time. Further, a black boy born in 1991 stood a 29 percent chance of being imprisoned at some point in his life, compared to a 16 percent chance for a Hispanic boy and a 4 percent chance for a white boy.

Figure 7-1

Lifetime Likelihood of Imprisonment for Males Born in 1991

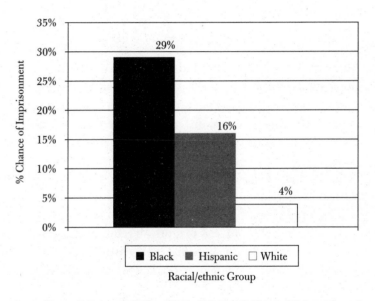

Source: Thomas P. Bonczar and Allen J. Beck, "Lifetime Likelihood of Going to State of Federal Prison," Bureau of Justice Statistics, 1997

For black women, the absolute numbers were not quite as overwhelming, but the trends were at least as disturbing. From 1985 to 1995, there was a 204 percent growth in the number of black women in federal and state prisons, considerably greater even than the 143 percent increase for black males or the 126 percent increase in the overall inmate population.

As if this weren't enough, leading academics, political pundits, and members of Congress began to refer to this new generation of criminals as containing a group of "superpredators." The animal imagery is inescapable here; consider whether most people conjure up the image of a white teenager when thinking of a "superpredator." Hardly. But a baggy pants–wearing black kid with a handgun fits the bill perfectly. To many Americans, some combination of bad family, bad culture, or bad genes created this young thug whose behavior is presumably beyond the capacity of modern law or social science to improve.

RACIAL DISPARITY AND IMPRISONMENT

Since whites are in effect "underrepresented" in the prison population—that is, in a smaller proportion than in the population as a whole—the black/white differential in incarceration is a ratio of more than seven to one. African Americans, therefore, have a seven times greater chance of being incarcerated than do whites.

In itself, this disparity does not tell us much. It is possible that African Americans commit seven times as much crime as whites, or perhaps seven times the rate of the more serious crimes that are likely to lead to a prison term. If that were the case, then one might conclude that the numbers in prison were related to social or economic factors, not that they are evidence of direct discrimination.

If we are to understand the means by which the disparities in imprisonment have developed, five areas of inquiry are most relevant: crime rates; criminal histories; racial bias in prosecution and sentencing; racial bias in responses to crime; and, criminal justice policy changes and their impact on African Americans.

1. Crime Rates

All things being equal, the most relevant factors that determine whether an offender will be sentenced to prison are the severity of the offense for which he or she is convicted and the offender's prior record. Thus, if African Americans exhibit higher rates of violent offending and/or have lengthier criminal histories than other groups, we would expect this to be reflected in the composition of the prison population.

For property crimes, African Americans constituted 32 percent of arrests in 1996, disproportionate to their share of the overall population. For violent crimes, though, black offending rates are considerably higher than for other groups, accounting for 43 percent of these arrests in 1996. As noted, arrest rates do not always correlate with crime rates (particularly for drug offenses), but they do provide a benchmark by which to assess criminal activity. While these arrest ratios are disturbing, they have remained stable for twenty years; the black proportion has fluctuated in a narrow range of 43–47 percent.[10] (This is clearly a very different picture than one would gather from watching only the eleven-o'clock news on television. Even during the upsurge of black juvenile homicides in the late 1980s, a declining rate of homicide among black adults resulted in a stable rate overall for African Americans.)

The degree to which arrest rates may explain the racial composition of the prison population has been examined by criminologist Alfred Blumstein in two separate studies of the 1979 and 1991 state prison populations.[11] Blumstein found that, with the critical exception of drug offenses, higher rates of crime (as measured by arrests) were responsible for most of the high rate of black incarceration. In the 1991 study, for example, he found that 76 percent of the higher black rate of imprisonment was accounted for by higher rates of arrest. The remaining 24 percent of disparity might be explained by racial bias or other factors.

The 24 percent figure may be alarming in itself. Suppose just 5 percent of the total incarceration were the result of racial bias: of the approximately 500,000 African American state prison inmates in 1995, about 25,000 would not be locked up absent this bias.

As Blumstein acknowledges, we need to be cautious as well about interpreting the remaining 76 percent of the black rate of imprisonment explained by higher arrest rates. For drug offenses in particular, as we shall see in detail in the next chapter, there is strong evidence that blacks are arrested far out of proportion of their actual use or sale of drugs. Therefore, as drug offenders represent a greater share of the prison population, the increased likelihood that blacks will be arrested and incarcerated for a drug offense means that a declining proportion of the prison population can be explained by higher rates of crime.

In another examination of the impact of arrest rates on incarceration in the 1980s, sociologists Robert Crutchfield, George Bridges, and Susan Pitchford found that at a national level, higher black arrest rates accounted for 89.5 percent of racial disparity in imprisonment. As in the Blumstein studies, these authors used arrests as a proxy for crime rates. At the state level, though, the amount of disparity that could be explained by arrests varied significantly. In the northeast states, only 69 percent of racial disparity was accounted for by arrest, while in the north central states, fewer blacks were actually incarcerated than one would have predicted by just using arrest data.[12] Overall, this suggests that a variety of factors, which may include crime rates, law enforcement priorities, and sentencing legislation, may play a role in the degree of racial disparity in incarceration.

2. Criminal Histories

Prior criminal history is generally considered to be another explanation for some of the disparity in rates of imprisonment. Of course, whether one acquires a criminal record is itself very much a function of race, geographical location, and other factors.

For example, in recent years, many African Americans have become acquainted with the crime known as "Driving While Black." In different parts of the country, there is strong evidence regarding the propensity of police to stop black males while

driving for alleged traffic violations. Often, the justification offered for these actions, based on supposed drug courier "pro-
files," is that they are necessary for apprehending drug
traffickers. In Volusia County in central Florida, for example,
researchers documented traffic stops made by local police in the
late 1980s. More than 70 percent of all drivers stopped were either African American or Hispanic. For the state as a whole,
blacks constituted 12 percent of the driving age population and
15 percent of drivers convicted of traffic violations. Blacks and
Hispanics were also stopped for longer periods of time than
whites, and represented 80 percent of the cars that were
searched following a stop.[13] To the extent that some drivers of
all races may possess drugs or other illegal goods, traffic stops
that disproportionately affect minorities will also detect a disproportionate number of minority offenders.

3. Racial Bias in Prosecution and Sentencing

Few honest observers of the criminal justice system would contend that race never played a role in determining rates of conviction and incarceration. Nonetheless, some observers do suggest
that in the modern era, racially biased decision-making has effectively been removed from the criminal justice system or at
least does not play a significant role. Thus, we see academic
texts with titles such as *The Myth of a Racist Criminal Justice
System*, citing statistical evidence to argue that race plays no significant factor in how offenders are treated in the system.[14]
These presentations generally fail to consider how the criminal
justice system has come to operate in such an unbiased manner
when bias is still frequently encountered in other institutions.

In fact, the influence of race can be seen very clearly in some
areas of the criminal justice system. Death penalty sentences
provide the most compelling evidence. A series of studies demonstrates that, controlling for a wide range of variables, the race
of both victim and offender has a significant impact on the determination of a sentence of death as opposed to life in prison.

David Baldus and colleagues, for example, found that murder defendants charged with killing whites faced a 4.3 times greater chance of receiving death than those charged with killing blacks.[15]

In one of the more remarkable rulings of the Supreme Court, the 1987 *McCleskey v. Kemp* decision upheld the constitutionality of these outcomes.[16] Warren McCleskey, a black man convicted of the armed robbery of a furniture store and the killing of a white police officer in the course of the robbery, argued that since race has an overwhelming influence on the imposition of the death penalty, his sentence should be overturned. While not quarreling with the statistical evidence presented by McCleskey, the court ruled that overall statistical evidence of discrimination could not be presumed to necessarily have affected his particular case. In other words, patterns of statistical racial disparities were meaningless unless one could show specific evidence of discrimination based on race.

Such a determination is, of course, virtually impossible. Prosecutors do not state in court, nor do they necessarily believe, that they are seeking the death penalty because a black defendant killed a white person, nor do judges offer this as their rationale for imposing the death penalty. In fact, it is far more likely that in the late twentieth century, in contrast to earlier times, patterns of discrimination reflect *unconscious* biases rather than blatant attempts to oppress African Americans.

Troublingly, the Supreme Court justices revealed a fear of opening up the sensitive issue of racial disparities in sentencing to public debate.[17] What would be the consequence, the majority in the McCleskey case asked, of permitting this type of challenge? Would it throw "into serious question the principles that underlie our entire criminal justice system?"[18] Would it also lead to claims challenging "unexplained discrepancies that correlate to membership in other minority groups and even to gender?"[19] Perhaps burglars and other common criminals would then be free to contest their sentences due to racial bias? In his dissent, Justice Brennan writes that the majority's reasoning "seems to suggest a fear of too much justice."[20]

While race clearly does play a role in some sentencing decisions, the mechanism by which it operates is more subtle than in previous times. In recent years, a variety of studies conducted on sentencing practices have attempted to establish whether minorities receive harsher sentences than whites. A number of these studies have found little difference in sentences meted out when controlling for relevant variables, particularly the severity of the offense and the offender's prior record. A 1990 RAND study, for example, concluded that offenders in California received generally comparable sentences regardless of race for most offenses.[21] The one exception was in the area of drug sentences, a distinction we will turn to in more detail later.

Other research illuminates the complexity of these findings. One of the most sophisticated studies examined case processing and sentencing outcomes for persons arrested for a felony offense in New York State for the years 1990–92. Controlling for factors that included prior criminal history, gender, and county, the researchers found that for the more serious offenses there was relatively little difference in the sentences handed out—although it was estimated that 300 black and Hispanic offenders who received prison terms would not have had they been white. But for property offenses and misdemeanors, minorities were considerably more likely to receive jail terms, resulting in an additional 4,000 sentences a year for minorities statewide.[22] Similar results have been found in a study of felony sentencing in Detroit, where race had a significant effect on incarceration decisions in the less serious cases.[23]

The key reason for these findings may lie in the use of discretion by the courts when sentencing offenders. Violent offenders regardless of their race or ethnicity are quite likely to be sentenced to prison. But for less serious offenders—for whom there is an option but no *obligation* to sentence to prison—prosecutors and judges make decisions in each case about whether an offender will receive six months in jail, for example, or be required to enter a treatment program and make restitution to a victim.

It would be a mistake simply to attribute the results of such studies to prosecutorial and judicial racist beliefs; in some jurisdictions a significant number of prosecutors and judges are minorities prosecuting and sentencing other minorities to terms of incarceration. The results instead stem from reasons that are various and subtle. Do white offenders bring greater resources, such as a private defense attorney, with them to court to convince decision-makers that a jail or prison term is not warranted? Do whites have greater access to expert psychiatric testimony, or can they afford to subsidize placement in a substance abuse treatment program? Or, is unconscious racism at play: do whites speak in a language and manner that is more comfortable to the decision-makers in the courtroom?

4. Racial Bias in Responses to Crime

One final problem associated with statistical analyses of the role of race in sentencing relates to the underlying assumptions behind sentencing policies themselves. In many jurisdictions around the country, minorities constitute two thirds or more of the defendants in many offense categories. To what extent are "get tough" sentencing policies a reflection of the race and ethnicity of those likely to be affected by such policies? As the hue of the defendant population changes, do legislators and judges set different sentencing standards?

A recent study examined this issue by looking at changes in state prison populations between 1971 and 1991 and the factors that might be responsible for these trends.[24] The study concluded that by 1990, controlling for a variety of factors, the size of a state's black population was an even stronger predictor of the prison population than the rate of violent crime. The authors suggest that while these findings may reflect large-scale bias within the criminal justice system, they may also be a result of harsher sentencing policies and a greater commitment to prison construction in states with larger black populations. The way in which officials employ different responses to offenders can be seen in the massive outbreak of criminal activity that occurs every year on April 15th. Millions of (presumably) otherwise law-abiding middle-class citizens file their tax returns with various embellishments. Some exaggerate the extent of their charitable contributions, others their business or childcare expenses. The vast majority of these infractions are never detected because the system assumes taxpayer honesty and the enforcement mechanisms are weak. For those violators who are detected, the matter is usually handled administratively. The offender is called into the IRS office and sternly told that he or she must pay the taxes due plus a stiff fine. Only in the most exceptional of circumstances are criminal prosecution and incarceration even contemplated.

The history of marijuana policy provides another example. In the first several decades of the 1900s, marijuana was perceived as a drug used only by blacks and Mexican Americans, with references to use by jazz artists in nightclubs in the "racy" parts of town. Malcolm X tells us in his autobiography of his frequent use during his hipster days. Harry Anslinger, head of the Federal Bureau of Narcotics for three decades, even kept a file on "Marijuana and Musicians." Whether or not this perception was wholly accurate, it no doubt contributed to such policies as the Boggs Act of the 1950s, penalizing first-time possession of marijuana or heroin with a sentence of two to five years in prison.[25]

By the 1960s, though, marijuana began to be widely used by the white middle class. College campuses were flooded with youthful pot smokers, often flaunting their defiance of the law with "smoke-ins" and other public activities. As many of these young people and others were arrested for marijuana offenses, public attitudes began to change quickly. Commissions established by Presidents Kennedy and Johnson questioned the prevailing assumption of a direct link between marijuana and

violent crime or heroin use. Marijuana thus came to be perceived as a relatively harmless drug, one that was not addictive
and did not particularly lead to other criminal behavior. By
1970, the Comprehensive Drug Abuse Prevention and Control
Act differentiated marijuana from other narcotics and lowered
federal penalties for possession of small amounts. Many states
and localities began to revise their marijuana laws and policies;
some jurisdictions all but decriminalized possession of small
quantities, either through new statutes or deliberately lax law
enforcement.

Even with these changes, differences in marijuana laws and
enforcement policies continue, often with consequences for
continuing racial disparity. In the city of Milwaukee, for example, possession of marijuana for many years was classified as
a misdemeanor, whereas the same behavior in the suburbs was
treated as an ordinance violation. Thus, the mostly nonwhite
arrests in the city could result in jail time and a criminal record,
while white offenders in the suburbs were issued a ticket and
made to pay a fine.[26]

The point here is not whether one believes that marijuana is a
dangerous drug or not; rather, it is how the public perception of
the appropriate societal response was shaped by the composition of the user population. As whites became a larger proportion of the user population and replaced blacks in the public
image of the pot user, public policies changed rapidly in a more
understanding and less punitive direction.

A study that a colleague and I conducted on societal responses to different forms of substance abuse illustrates this as
well. The study examined the harm to society and the criminal
justice response to two forms of substance abuse, drunk driving
and drug possession.[27] Both forms of substance abuse result in
substantial numbers of arrests (1.8 million for drunk driving in
1990 and 700,000 for drug possession), as well as significant
societal harm, which can be approximated by examining the
number of deaths caused by each.

As of 1990, drunk drivers were responsible for approximately 22,000 deaths annually, while overall alcohol-related deaths approached 100,000 a year. Drug-related deaths, through overdose, AIDS, or the violence associated with the drug trade, were estimated at 21,000 annually.

In response to increasing concern about drunk driving and due to the efforts of advocacy groups such as Mothers Against Drunk Driving, most states adopted stiffer laws to punish drunk driving in the 1980s. Many states now have some form of mandatory sentencing for this offense, although this typically involves two days for a first offense and 2–10 days for a second offense. Often, a convicted drunk driver is permitted to perform community service rather than serve a jail term.

The "war on drugs," though, has dramatically increased the number of drug arrests and made sentencing provisions harsher in most states. Drug possession arrests rose by 88 percent in the period 1980–90. Typical state penalties for drug possession (excluding marijuana) are up to 5 years for a first offense and 1–10 years for a second offense.

Who are the individuals arrested for these offenses? Drunk drivers are predominantly white males, representing 78 percent of the arrests for this offense as of 1990. They are generally charged as misdemeanants and typically receive sentences involving fines, license suspension, and community service. Persons convicted of drug possession, though, are disproportionately low-income, and African American or Hispanic; they are usually charged with felonies and frequently sentenced to incarceration. Overall, the societal response to drunk drivers has generally emphasized keeping the person functional and in society, while attempting to respond to the dangerous behavior through treatment; for drug offenders, though, the response has primarily involved greater use of law enforcement and incarceration. At the same time, while drug treatment remains popular and available for middle-class drug users, it is in short supply for low-income persons.

We have already seen how sentencing practices in Western Europe are less harsh for some offenses than in the United

States. In comparing the United States with Scandinavian nations, for example, many skeptics contend that the relatively humane sentencing policies of Scandinavia are due to the fact that these societies are more homogeneous. Precisely! Communities that feel a sense of commitment to their members are able to see the humanity of offenders despite their criminal behaviors and to see the potential for positive change in their lives.

5. Policy Changes and African Americans

Unlike in South Africa under apartheid or the pre-Civil Rights South, criminal justice policies of the past several decades in the United States have not consciously targeted the African American community for particularly harsh treatment. By failing to forecast the likely impact of criminal justice policies, though — that is, in not attempting to understand what should have been some very predictable outcomes — policymakers have been derelict.

The advent of the "get tough" movement in the 1970s in itself was bound to have a disproportionate impact on minority communities. With African Americans already representing 40 percent of the prison population in 1970, a doubling of the prison population was likely to have a substantial impact on the absolute number of imprisoned minorities, absent some dramatic changes in crime rates or criminal justice processing decisions.

A more profoundly consequential policy change was the shift from indeterminate to determinate sentencing. This change was the result not only of the "get tough" movement, but, as we've noted, concern regarding the potential for abuse of discretion inherent in any indeterminate sentencing system. Reformers believed that controlling this discretion would lessen disparities based on race or class.

In its milder forms, determinate sentencing took on the form of sentencing guidelines that kept judicial discretion within acceptable bounds but permitted departures for compelling reasons. Some of the state guidelines systems appear to have reduced, but not eliminated, unwarranted racial disparity.[28]

The more restrictive versions of determinate sentencing included the federal sentencing guidelines that took effect in 1987 and the host of mandatory sentencing laws that removed judicial discretion for many drug and weapons offenses. Under the political slogan of "if you do the crime, you'll do the time," mandatory sentences held out the promise of certainty in punishment regardless of who the offender was. Theoretically, this could have led to reduced disparity in sentencing.

Theory bore only a slight relation to courtroom reality, though, because it was dependent on the notion that discretion could somehow be eliminated from the sentencing process. What seems to have been forgotten in this calculation was that the entire criminal justice process is predicated on the use of discretion. A whole host of decisions guide criminal justice actors — where police officers will patrol, whether to arrest kids who are drinking underage or to inform their parents, whether to charge a shoplifting offense as a misdemeanor or a felony, whether to offer a plea or go to trial, and so on.

Legislators who trumpeted their support of mandatory sentencing also overlooked the critical role of the prosecutor in the sentencing process. While mandatory sentencing might require the judge to impose a certain sentence, it said nothing about how a prosecutor would charge a case, negotiate a plea, or make a recommendation on sentencing.

In many cases, prosecutors might offer a defendant charged with a drug offense carrying a mandatory five-year prison term a plea bargain to a lesser charge, carrying only two years of imprisonment upon conviction. Is this done because the prosecutor is "softer on crime" than the legislators who supported mandatory sentencing? Hardly. Rather, it represents the prosecutor's understanding of the reality of the courtroom process, which would collapse under its own weight were most cases not negotiated.

So discretion has not been eliminated from the system; rather, it has been transferred from the judge to the prosecutor. The implications of this movement for democracy are crucial:

judicial discretion is exercised in an open courtroom subject to public scrutiny, but the exercise of prosecutorial discretion is conducted behind closed doors with little accountability.

One comprehensive examination of prosecutorial decision-making was an analysis of case processing conducted by the *San Jose Mercury News*. The study looked at 700,000 criminal cases that were matched by crime and criminal history of the defendant. The analysts concluded that "at virtually every stage of pretrial negotiation, whites are more successful than non-whites."[29] Of 71,000 adults with no prior record who were arrested on felony charges, one third of the whites had charges reduced to misdemeanors or infractions, while only one quarter of blacks and Hispanics received this disposition.

How these dynamics come about has been the subject of considerable speculation by scholars. It may be that prosecutorial bias is reflected in an unwillingness to offer favorable plea agreements to minorities; another possibility is that minority defendants may be less trusting of the system and therefore less willing to engage in the plea-bargaining process.

Bias may also play a role in the degree to which cases are vigorously pursued by the prosecution. A review of research in this area conducted by sociologists John Hagan and Ruth Peterson suggests that prosecutors stereotype cases according to case-specific characteristics, by making racially biased assessments of the credibility of the victim and offender as witnesses. Nonwhite victims tend to be considered less credible witnesses, while white victims, especially of nonwhite defendants, are considered highly credible.[30] Given that most crime is intraracial, committed against victims of the same race, these dynamics may actually benefit black defendants but penalize black victims in some cases.

Several studies have attempted to measure evidence of racial disparities resulting from or continuing under mandatory sentencing laws in the federal court system. A report by the Federal Judicial Center found that in 1990 blacks were 21 percent more likely and Hispanics 28 percent more likely than whites to receive a mandatory prison term for offense behavior that fell under the mandatory sentencing legislation.[31] A more comprehensive statistical analysis by the United States Sentencing Commission concluded that, for comparable behavior, whites were being offered plea bargains leading to outcomes falling below the level requiring a mandatory minimum sentence more often than blacks or Hispanics although a reexamination by an analyst for the Justice Department concluded that these disparities were based on legally relevant case-processing factors.[32]

A close look at the federal sentencing guidelines themselves also suggests the difficulty of eliminating nonracial forms of bias in the system. One of the original justifications for the guidelines was the intent to eliminate favored treatment for wealthier defendants. A doctor convicted of Medicaid fraud, for example, would no longer be able to offer to donate his medical services to the community as a means of escaping a stay in prison.

The first problem with this approach is its assumption that the justice system will pursue the crimes of the wealthy as zealously as those of the poor. There is little evidence that this has ever been the case. Even if this were true, there is a basic flaw in the premise that incarceration, rather than a nonprison sanction, should be the presumptive penalty for most offenders. Rather than exploring whether the community service and treatment sentences that white-collar offenders had received might be appropriate for at least some low-income offenders, the guideline promulgators decreed that virtually all offenders should go to prison.

Second, the sentencing guidelines create sharp restrictions on the background issues a judge is permitted to take into account at sentencing. This injures low-income and minority offenders more than wealthy ones. Sentencing Commission guidelines, for example, forbid reductions in sentence for "lack of guidance as a youth and similar circumstances indicating a disadvantaged upbringing."[33]

Narrowing judicial allowance for mitigating factors has had a significant impact on women offenders, too Law professor Myrna Raeder's analysis of federal sentencing concludes that the development of guidelines often assumes a "male" norm.[34] Women have traditionally received the benefit of consideration for having a secondary role in the commission of a crime or a history of sexual or physical abuse. But when prior sentencing patterns—primarily based on male offenders—are calculated, these factors are now deemed largely irrelevant

Thus, the sentencing policies of recent years, whether motivated by a desire to "get tough" or to reduce disparity, have in fact unfairly affected low-income people and minorities. Had these been the only changes in criminal justice policy, the impact would have been regrettable enough. The inauguration of the "war on drugs," though, made these policies pale in significance.

NOTES

1. Nkechi Taifa, "Laying Down the Law, Race by Race," *Legal Times*, Oct. 10, 1994.
2. Darnell Hawkins, "Crime and Ethnicity," in Brian Forst, ed., *The Socio-economics of Crime and Justice* (Armonk, N.Y.: M. E. Sharpe, 1993), p. 98.
3. David M. Oshinsky, *Worse Than Slavery* (New York: Free Press, 1996), p. 32.
4. Ibid., p. 44.
5. Ibid., p. 46.
6. The Bureau of Justice Statistics reports that not all states participated in the 1926 reporting, but that this does not affect the overall trends observed.
7. Michael Radelet and Margaret Vandiver, "Race and Capital Punishment: An Overview of the Issues," *Crime and Social Justice* 25 (1986), p. 98.
8. Elliott Currie, *Confronting Crime* (New York: Pantheon Books, 1985), pp. 110–111.
9. Jock Young, "Writing on the Cusp of Change: A New Criminology for an Age of Late Modernity," in Paul Walton and Jock Young, eds., *The New Criminology Revisited* (London: Macmillan, 1998), pp. 259–95.
10. Michael Tonry, *Malign Neglect: Race, Crime, and Punishment in America* (New York: Oxford University Press, 1995), p. 64.
11. Alfred Blumstein, "On the Racial Disproportionality of United States' Prison Populations," *Journal of Criminal Law and Criminology* 73 (1982), pp. 1259–81; Alfred Blumstein, "Racial Disproportionality of U.S. Prison Populations Revisited," *University of Colorado Law Review* 64 (1993), pp. 743–60.
12. Robert D. Crutchfield, George S. Bridges, and Susan R. Pitchford, "Analytical and Aggregation Biases in Analyses of Imprisonment: Reconciling Discrepancies in Studies of Racial Disparity," *Journal of Research in Crime and Delinquency* 31 (May 1994).

13. David A. Harris, " 'Driving While Black' and All Other Traffic Offenses: The Supreme Court and Pretextual Traffic Stops," *Journal of Criminal Law and Criminology* 87 (Summer 1997), p. 562.

14. William Wilbanks, *The Myth of a Racist Criminal Justice System* (Monterey, Calif.: Brooks/Cole, 1987).

15. David C. Baldus, Charles Pulaski, and George Woodworth, "Comparative Review of Death Sentences: An Empirical Study of the Georgia Experience," *Journal of Criminal Law and Criminology* 74 (Fall 1983), pp. 661–753.

16. *McCleskey v. Kemp*, 481 U.S. 279, 107 S. Ct. 1756.

17. I am indebted to Bryan Stevenson for pointing out the significance of this aspect of the ruling.

18. *McCleskey*, at 1779.

19. *McCleskey*, at 1780.

20. *McCleskey*, at 1791.

21. Stephen Klein, Joan Petersilia, and Susan Turner, "Race and Imprisonment Decisions in California," *Science* (Feb. 16, 1990).

22. James F. Nelson, *Disparities in Processing Felony Arrests in New York State, 1990–92* (Albany, N.Y.: Division of Criminal Justice Services, 1995).

23. Samuel Walker, Cassia Spohn, and Miriam DeLone, *The Color of Justice*, (Belmont, Calif.: Wadsworth, 1996), p. 165.

24. David F. Greenberg and Valerie West, "The Persistent Significance of Race: Growth in State Prison Populations, 1971–1991," paper presented to Law and Society Association, Aspen, Colorado, June 1998.

25. Eric Schlosser, "Reefer Madness," *Atlantic Monthly* (Aug. 1994), p. 49.

26. Jim Stingl, "Drug laws seen as factor in racial crime disparities," *Milwaukee Journal Sentinel*, April 3, 1997.

27. Cathy Shine and Marc Mauer, *Does the Punishment Fit the Crime? Drug Users and Drunk Drivers, Questions of Race and Class* (Washington, D.C.: The Sentencing Project, 1993).

28. Michael Tonry, *Sentencing Matters* (New York: Oxford University Press, 1995), p. 57.

29. Christopher Schmitt, "Plea bargaining favors whites, as blacks, Hispanics pay price," *San Jose Mercury News*, Dec. 8, 1991.

30. John Hagan and Ruth D. Peterson, "Criminal Inequality in America: Patterns and Consequences," in John Hagan and Ruth D. Peterson, *Crime and Inequality* (Stanford, Calif.: Stanford University Press, 1995), p. 28.

31. Barbara S. Meierhoefer, *The General Effect of Mandatory Minimum Prison Terms* (Washington, D.C.: Federal Judicial Center, 1992), p. 20.

32. Dale Parent, et al., *Mandatory Sentencing* (Washington, D.C.: National Institute of Justice, January 1997), p. 4.

33. Tonry, *Sentencing Matters*, p. 77.

34. Myrna Raeder, "Gender and Sentencing: Single Moms, Battered Women, and Other Sex-based Anomalies in the Gender-free World of the Federal Sentencing Guidelines," *Pepperdine Law Review* 20.3 (1993).

8—The War on Drugs and the African American Community

Sure, it's true we prosecute a high percentage of minorities for drugs. The simple fact is, if you have a population, minority or not, that is conducting most of their illegal business on the street, those cases are easy pickings for the police.

—Delaware Prosecutor Charles Butler[1]

Picture this scene in any middle-class suburb in the United States: students at the local high school, a "good" school with high graduation rates and college acceptances, have been getting into trouble. Nothing too serious, but some drug use, some underage drinking, and a few smashed cars here and there. Parents are cautioned by the principal to check with their kids for signs of trouble.

The parents of one 17-year-old boy had already been concerned about possible drug use, and examine their son's bedroom while he is at school. They discover what appears to be some drug residue and a substantial amount of cash hidden in a drawer. Confronting their son when he comes home, he admits he has been using cocaine and occasionally selling to some friends.

How do the parents respond? Do they call up the police, demand that their son be arrested for using and selling drugs, and receive a five-year mandatory minimum sentence for his behavior? The question is ludicrous, of course.

Instead, the parents do what any good middle-class family would do: they consult with their insurance provider and then secure the best treatment program they can find. The criminal justice system never even becomes an issue for them.

A few miles away, picture another family in a low-income section of the city. Their son, too, appears to be getting involved with drugs. Unfortunately for him, his parents have no health insurance, and there are few drug treatment programs available in the neighborhood. Finally, he is picked up one night on a street corner and charged with drug possession with the intent to sell.

Two families with substance abuse problems, two different responses. What does this tell us about the choices available to families and communities, and whether the criminal justice system need be the inevitable response to illegal behavior?

Since 1980, no policy has contributed more to the incarceration of African Americans than the "war on drugs." To say this is not to deny the reality of drug abuse and the toll it has taken on African American and other communities; but as a national policy, the drug war has exacerbated racial disparities in incarceration while failing to have any sustained impact on the drug problem.

DRUG USE AND DRUG ARRESTS

With nondrug street crimes, such as burglary or larceny, the police operate in a reactive mode: citizens report a crime and the police investigate. With drug selling or possession, though, there is no direct "victim"; consequently, no reports are made to the police (except possibly those made by complaining neighbors). Drug law enforcement is far more discretionary than for other offenses. The police decide when and where they will seek to make drug arrests, and most important, what priority they will place on enforcing drug laws.

The drug war's impact on the African American community can be mapped by looking at two overlapping trends. First, there has been an enormous increase in the number of drug arrests overall; second, African Americans have constituted an increasing proportion of those arrests.

As seen in Figure 8-1, in 1980 there were 581,000 arrests for drug offenses, a number that nearly doubled to 1,090,000 by 1990. Although it appeared for a while that these trends might be leveling off in the early 1990s with a decline in arrests, that

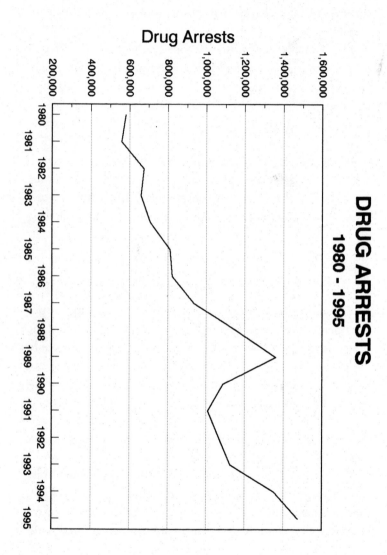

Figure 8-1
Drug Arrests, 1980–1995

Source: FBI data provided to the author

trend was quickly reversed: a record 1,476,000 drug arrests were made by 1995.[2]

Did these arrests reflect rising rates of drug abuse nationally? No. In fact, the best data available show that the number of people using drugs had been declining since 1979, when 14.1 percent of the population reported using drugs in the past month. This proportion had halved to 6.7 percent by 1990, and it declined to 6.1 percent by 1995.[3] Since fewer people were using drugs, and presumably fewer selling as well, then all things being equal, one would have thought that drug arrests would have declined as well.

But all things are not equal when it comes to crime and politics. Instead, heightened political and media attention, and increased budgets for law enforcement all contributed to a greater use of police resources to target drug offenders. At the same time, police increasingly began to target low-income minority communities for drug law enforcement.

We can see this most clearly by analyzing arrest data prepared annually by the FBI. As seen in Figure 8-2, in 1980, African Americans, who constitute 13 percent of the U.S. population, accounted for 21 percent of drug possession arrests nationally. This number rose to a high of 36 percent in 1992 before dropping somewhat to 33 percent by 1995. For juveniles, the figures are even more stark: although blacks represented 13 percent of juvenile drug possession arrests in 1980, this proportion climbed to 40 percent by 1991, before declining to 30 percent in 1995. In looking at these statistics, we might conclude that blacks began using drugs in greater numbers during the decade of the 1980s, thereby leading to their being arrested more frequently. Certainly, a glance at television newscasts or weekly newsmagazines would have given us this impression.

In fact, no such dramatic rise can be detected. The best data available on drug use is compiled by the Substance Abuse and Mental Health Services Administration (SAMHSA) of the Department of Health and Human Services, which conducts a household survey annually to prepare estimates on the extent of

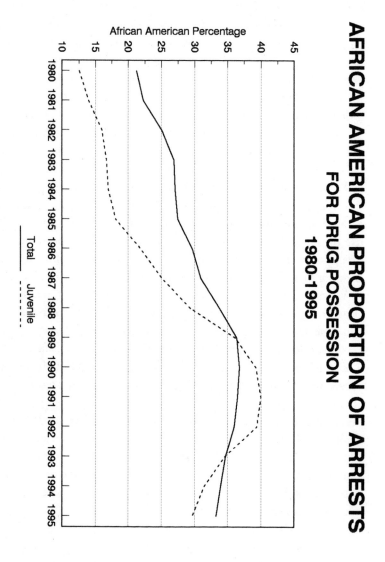

Figure 8-2
African American Proportion of Arrests for Drug Possession, 1980–1995

Source: FBI data provided to the author

drug use. Although these data cover 98 percent of the population, they have some limitations. Since this is by definition a household survey, anyone not living in a household will not be incorporated in the findings. Thus, prisoners, homeless persons not living in a shelter, and military personnel are not covered. Since minorities are disproportionately represented among these groups, they will therefore be underrepresented in the household survey. Nevertheless, the survey is generally regarded as the best portrait of the nation's drug-using population.

The SAMHSA surveys question individuals regarding drug use during the past month, past year, or ever in their lifetime. For our purposes, drug use during the past month is the most relevant piece of information, since frequent users are more likely to be arrested than infrequent ones.

Looking at the data for 1995, we find that while African Americans were slightly more likely to be monthly drug users than whites and Hispanics (7.9 percent vs. 6.0 percent and 5.1 percent respectively), the much greater number of whites in the overall population resulted in their constituting the vast majority of drug users. Thus, the SAMHSA data indicate that whites represented 77 percent of current drug users, with African Americans constituting 15 percent of users and Hispanics, 8 percent.[4] Even assuming that blacks may be somewhat undercounted in the household surveys, it is difficult to imagine that African American drug use is of a magnitude that could explain blacks representing 15 percent of current drug users yet 33 percent of arrests for drug possession.

Some observers have speculated that the higher arrest rates for drug possession may reflect the type of drug that is being used—in essence, law enforcement is more likely to target cocaine users or crack cocaine users. Unfortunately, FBI arrest data do not distinguish between powder cocaine and crack cocaine. Arrest data for all cocaine possession offenses for 1995 show that African Americans constituted 47 percent of all such arrests. Looking at data on cocaine use, though, we find that there are no dramatic differences in cocaine use by race or ethnicity. In 1995, 1.1 percent of blacks reported that they had used cocaine in the past month, compared to 0.7 percent of Hispanics and 0.6 percent of whites.[5] Overall, this translates into African Americans representing 18 percent of all recent cocaine users.

For users of crack cocaine, the disproportionate use among blacks is considerably higher than for cocaine overall, but it doesn't explain the arrest disparities. Data for 1995 show that although crack use is quite low for all groups, African Americans are six times as likely as whites to have used it in the past month and three times as likely as Hispanics (0.6 percent vs. 0.1 percent and 0.2 percent respectively).[6] Given the much greater proportion of whites in the overall population, though, these user rates translate into whites representing 54 percent of current crack users, blacks 34 percent and Hispanics 12 percent.

Are police arresting crack and cocaine users in general or preferentially going into black neighborhoods where some people are using these drugs? Conducting drug arrests in inner-city neighborhoods does have advantages for law enforcement. First, it is far easier to make arrests in such areas, since drug dealing is more likely to take place in open-air drug markets. In contrast, drug dealing in suburban neighborhoods almost invariably takes place behind closed doors and is therefore not readily identifiable to passing police. Second, because both drug use and dealing are more likely to take place openly, residents of African American neighborhoods are more likely to complain about these behaviors and to ask for police intervention. Since law enforcement has long been accused of failing to respond to problems of minority neighborhoods in a timely manner, many police departments are now more focused on attempting to remedy this problem—so they are likely to respond to complaints emanating from these neighborhoods.

Racial targeting by police may also have an effect on black neighborhoods that are not inner-city. Criminologists James Lynch and William Sabol analyzed data on incarceration rates, race, and class during the period 1979-91.[7] They identified inmates as either being "underclass" or "non-underclass" (working-class or middle class) based on educational levels, employment history, and income. They concluded that the most significant increase in incarceration rates was for working class black drug offenders, whose rates increased sixfold, from 1.5 per 1,000 in 1979 to match that of underclass blacks at 9 per 1,000 by 1991. The trend for whites, on the other hand, was just the opposite; the underclass drug incarceration rate was double that of the nonunderclass by 1991.

Lynch and Sabol suggest that two factors may explain these trends. First, law enforcement targeting of inner-city neighborhoods may initially sweep many underclass blacks into the criminal justice system. Second, due to residential racial segregation patterns, there may be a "spillover" effect whereby police increase the number of arrests in the working-class black neighborhoods that border underclass communities. They conclude that there has been

> an increased targeting of black working and middle class areas for discretionary drug enforcement and ultimately increased incarceration for drug offenses. The immunity that working and middle class status used to bring in the black community (and still does among whites) may have been lost. While the processes that produced these outcomes may not have been racially motivated in intent, they have resulted in racially disparate outcomes.[8]

DRUG SALES AND ARRESTS

Similar disproportionate arrest patterns can be seen for drug selling. In this area, the African American proportion rose from 35 percent in 1980 to 49 percent by 1995.

It is at least theoretically possible that the proportion of black drug traffickers has risen substantially in recent years, and that the arrest percentages reflect actual law-breaking behavior. However, as we examine these disparities we find that statistics on drug users are fairly irrelevant, since one can be a drug seller without being a user.[9] One means of addressing this problem is to look at responses to parts of the SAMHSA surveys in which respondents are asked whether it is "fairly or very easy" to obtain drugs in your neighborhood. Overall, 43 percent of the population in 1996 responded affirmatively regarding cocaine and 39 percent regarding crack. These figures, which document the relative ease of obtaining drugs after fifteen years of massive increase in the law enforcement resources devoted to the drug war, should give pause to those committed to such policies.

While blacks were more likely than whites to report that it was easy to obtain these drugs (57 percent vs. 43 percent for cocaine, and 58 percent vs. 38 percent for crack), the differences are still nowhere near the order of magnitude that would explain the arrest disparities.[10] A report issued by the Wisconsin Policy Research Institute, a conservative thinktank, provides part of the explanation in describing differences in the white suburban drug markets and inner-city black and Hispanic neighborhoods of Milwaukee.[11] While drug dealing was prevalent in each of the communities, the inner-city sales tended to be neighborhood-based, often taking place on street corners. In contrast, the suburban distribution of cocaine and other drugs took place by word of mouth through contacts at work, bars, athletic leagues, and alternative cultural events such as "raves." Suburban sales locations were more hidden from law enforcement than were those in the inner-city neighborhoods, but they were "not very difficult to locate," in the words of the author.

A 1997 report of the National Institute of Justice lends support to the fact that whites are frequently involved in selling drugs. In an analysis of drug transactions in six cities, the researchers found that "respondents were most likely to report using a main source who was of their own racial or ethnic background."[12]

Finally, consider the patterns of daily life in urban areas. If it were true that the overwhelming number of drug dealers are black, we would see large numbers of drug-seeking whites streaming into Harlem, South Central Los Angeles, and the east side of Detroit day after day. While some do visit these neighborhoods, there are few reports of massive numbers doing so on a regular basis. As Barry McCaffrey, director of the White House Office of National Drug Control Policy, has stated, if your child bought drugs, "it was from a student of their own race generally."[13]

SENTENCING FOR DRUG OFFENSES

The overrepresentation of African Americans in the criminal justice system has been exacerbated by changes in sentencing policy that coincided with the current drug war. Since 1975, every state has passed some type of mandatory sentencing law requiring incarceration for weapons offenses, habitual offenders, or other categories. These statutes have been applied most frequently to drug offenses, with two primary effects. First, they increase the proportion of arrested drug offenders who are sentenced to prison and, second, they increase the length of time that offenders serve in prison.

Data from the Bureau of Justice Statistics show that the chances of receiving a prison term after being arrested for a drug offense increased by 447 percent between 1980 and 1992.[14] A good portion of this increase was likely related to the requirement of mandatory sentencing, although no breakdown is available. Part of the increase may have also been a result of generally harsher attitudes toward drug offenders—that is, prosecutors and judges responding to a political climate increasingly punitive in its orientation toward drugs.

The impact of mandatory drug laws can be seen most dramatically in the federal court system. Drug offenders released from prison in 1990, many of whom had not been sentenced under mandatory provisions, had served an average of 30 months in prison. But offenders sentenced to prison in 1990—most of whom were subject to mandatory penalties—were expected to serve more than twice that term, or an average of 66 months.[15] This fact, combined with a greatly increased number of federal drug prosecutions, has resulted in the proportion of federal prisoners who are drug offenders increasing from 25 percent in 1980 to 60 percent by 1995.

At the state level, the longer prison terms brought about by mandatory sentencing laws have also had a significant impact on African Americans. Between 1985 and 1995, the average time served in prison for drug offenses rose by 20 percent from 20 months to 24 months.[16] Overall, the number of drug offenders in prison increased by 478 percent during this period, compared to a rise of 119 percent for all offenses.

A substantial portion of this increase consists of African Americans. This can be seen in Table 8-1. From 1985 to 1995, drug offenders constituted 42 percent of the rise in the black state prison population. Note here that drug offenders in this case refers to individuals convicted only of a drug offense and not, for example, a drug-*related* assault or robbery. For white offenders, by contrast, drug offenders represented 26 percent of the increase and violent offenders 42 percent. Overall, the number of white drug offenders increased by 306 percent in the ten-year period, while for blacks the increase was 707 percent.

The combined impact of law enforcement and sentencing policies on minorities is even more startling in some states. A 1997 study of drug law enforcement in Massachusetts found that blacks were 39 times more likely to be incarcerated for a drug offense than whites.[17] And the impact of drug policies on black women has been even more dramatic than for black men. In just the five-year period 1986–91, the number of black women incarcerated in state prison for a drug offense rose by 828 percent. Although the absolute numbers of women drug offenders in the system are considerably lower than for men, the trend is clearly disturbing.

Besides mandatory sentencing, other drug policies that may have been well intended have contributed to the alarming trends in black incarceration. One such policy is the set of drug laws that increase penalties for offenders who sell drugs near schools

Table 8-1

State Prison Inmates by Race and Offense

Offense	White				Black			
	1985	1995	% Increase	% Total Increase	1985	1995	% Increase	% Total Increase
Total	224,900	471,100	109 %	100 %	211,100	490,100	132 %	100 %
Violent	111,900	214,800	92 %	42 %	124,800	228,600	83 %	37 %
Drug	21,200	86,100	306 %	26 %	16,600	134,000	707 %	42 %
Property	75,100	130,700	74 %	23 %	60,600	100,200	65 %	14 %
Public Order	14,900	39,000	162 %	10 %	7,600	25,000	229 %	6 %
Other	1,800	500	−72 %	−1 %	1,400	2,300	64 %	0 %

Source: Christopher J. Mumola and Allen J. Beck, "Prisoners in 1996," Bureau of Justice Statistics, June 1997

or public housing. Ostensibly, the goal is to establish "drug-free" zones that are safe for children and other residents. As a University of Chicago law professor reminds us:

> . . . in Illinois, a fifteen-year-old first-time offender charged with selling a controlled substance within 1,000 feet of public housing is treated as an adult. In contrast, a fifteen-year-old first-time offender charged with selling a controlled substance from or near his home in the suburbs is treated as a juvenile. Counseling, treatment, and targeted programs are made available to the juvenile suburbanite while the inner city youth most in need of social services enters the resource starved adult criminal justice system.[18]

Bobbie Marshall, an African American who has used drugs since his teens, experienced the impact of this kind of law following his arrest for selling drugs within 1,000 feet of a school in Los Angeles. Because of his three prior convictions for selling small quantities of drugs to feed his habit, Marshall faced the possibility of life without parole under a federal statute. Marshall's attorneys documented that 89 of 90 persons arrested under a joint state/federal task force in the "schoolyard program" were either African American or Hispanic.

By the time of Marshall's sentencing, he had in many ways turned his life around. He had become active in counseling gang members, helped keep the peace during the 1992 Los Angeles riots, and remained drug free. His efforts led to letters of support from ministers, a police commander, a congressman, and others. Although the prosecution eventually agreed to a nine-year term for Marshall, the sentencing judge imposed only half that term, arguing that Marshall's rehabilitation and value to the community were exceptional. Under the federal mandatory sentencing laws, though, the judge was overruled on appeal.

The most discussed reason for the racial disparity in drug sentencing in recent years has been the issue of sentencing for crack cocaine offenses. As crack made its entry into urban areas in the mid-1980s, reports began to surface about this new highly addictive and powerful drug. Cover stories appeared in *Newsweek*, *Time*, and periodicals around the country. Reports of "crack babies" born to addicted mothers were among the most frightening to surface. How could anyone fail to respond to this human tragedy? Only later did information surface that indicated that there were in fact no data on crack-addicted babies.

Testing cannot distinguish between prenatal exposure to crack cocaine and powder cocaine, so there is no way to know how many of these mothers had in fact used crack while pregnant. Further, the children of drug-abusing mothers who develop poorly may in fact be suffering from a combination of factors that often correlate with low-income drug abusing mothers, including poor nutrition, smoking, and lack of prenatal care. A study by researchers at the Albert Einstein Medical Center in Philadelphia tracked the development of more than 200 low-income inner-city children, half of whom had been exposed to cocaine in the womb and half not. The study found that both groups of children scored below average on IQ tests and other measures of cognitive development, but that there was no significant difference between the two groups.[19] Clearly, any type of substance abuse by pregnant women is unhealthy for both mother and child. In this instance, though, the image of "crack babies" had a significant impact on subsequent legislation.

Crack, of course, is a dangerous drug; its use has caused real destruction to many individuals and communities. The extent of this harm and any realistic assessment of possible responses, though, were hardly considered by Congress in its rush to adopt harsh "antidrug" penalties in 1986 and again in 1988. The mandatory sentencing laws passed by Congress provided for far harsher punishments for crack offenses than for powder cocaine crimes. Thus, the sale of 500 grams of cocaine powder resulted in a mandatory five-year prison term, while only 5 grams of crack was required to trigger the same mandatory penalty.

In addition to the other racial dynamics of the drug war, these laws have had a major impact on African Americans. The vast majority of persons charged with crack trafficking offenses in the federal system—88 percent in 1992–93—have been African American.[20] Federal prosecutors contend that these figures merely reflect the proportions of large-scale traffickers in crack who qualify for federal prosecution because of their substantial role in the drug trade. Data analyzed by the U.S. Sentencing Commission, though, casts doubt on this contention: in the Commission's analysis of crack defendants in 1992, only 5.5 percent of the defendants were classified as high-level dealers, while 63.7 percent were considered street-level dealers or couriers, and 30.8 percent mid-level dealers.[21]

Given the severity of crack penalties in the federal system, the prosecutorial decision regarding whether to charge a drug offense as a state or federal crime has potentially significant consequences for sentencing. The results of a *Los Angeles Times* analysis, which examined prosecutions for crack cocaine trafficking in the Los Angeles area from 1988 to 1994, are quite revealing.[22] During that period, not a single white offender was convicted of a crack offense in federal court, despite the fact that whites comprise a majority of crack users. During the same period, though, hundreds of white crack traffickers were prosecuted in state courts, often receiving sentences as much as eight years less than those received by offenders in federal courts. As is true nationally, the *Times* analysis revealed that many of the African Americans charged in federal court were not necessarily drug kingpins, but rather low-level dealers or accomplices in the drug trade.

The folly of using expensive prison space for drug offenders, even traffickers, has been documented in research conducted on the federal prison population. One study examined costs and recidivism for low-level drug traffickers in the federal prison system before and after the imposition of mandatory prison terms.[23] It found that over half of the offenders sentenced to prison in 1992 were drug traffickers. Of these, 62 percent, or 9,000 offenders, were considered low-risk as defined by their limited criminal histories. The study then examined recidivism rates for a comparable group of 236 offenders released from prison in 1987, prior to the adoption of mandatory minimums and the federal sentencing guidelines. It found that only 19 percent of the low-risk drug traffickers were re-arrested during the three years after release, and that none of those arrested were charged with serious crimes of violence.

In contrast, the low-risk traffickers sentenced to prison in 1992 were expected to serve three years longer in prison than the 1987 release group (51 months vs. 17 months). The study concluded that the additional time spent in prison for the 9,000 offenders would cost taxpayers approximately $515 million.

Similar findings have been documented regarding the relatively minor roles and criminal histories of drug offenders in state prisons. A report published by the Urban Institute provided an analysis of the more than 150,000 drug offenders incarcerated in state prisons in 1991.[24] Almost 127,000 of these offenders, or 84 percent, had no history of a prior incarceration for a violent crime, and one half of the offenders had no prior incarcerations at all. One third of the drug offenders sentenced to state prison had been convicted of the less serious possession offenses—hardly a qualification for a high-level player in the drug trade.

The Urban Institute analysis further documents that the increased incarceration of drug offenders has contributed to a rise in the imprisonment of what has been termed "socially integrated offenders"—in other words, there has been a rise in the proportion of inmates who have ties to legitimate institutions such as families, education, and labor markets. Between 1979 and 1991, for example, the number of state prison inmates with some college education rose from 10,000 to 44,000, and the number employed prior to their incarceration increased from 192,000 to 476,000.[25] The Urban Institute authors contend that the incarceration of socially integrated offenders "may be unnecessary because prior experience has shown that socially integrated people are less likely to re-offend. Such people can, therefore, be punished by means other than incarceration without putting the public at undue risk." Further, by reducing ties to legitimate institutions, incarceration may make these offenders "more prone to subsequent criminal involvement."[26]

OPTIONS IN DRUG POLICY

Some political leaders and others contend that drug laws and the way they are implemented are unbiased, and that higher black rates of selling and using drugs are responsible for any discrepancies. Rep. Bill McCollum, Republican of Florida and the chair of the House Judiciary Committee, for example, has stated that "the [crack cocaine] mandatory sentences are the same for black and white people. More African Americans generally get caught up with crime and wind up doing things that put them in jail for longer periods of time. But that doesn't have anything to do with discrimination."[27]

A more sophisticated critique is offered by law professor Randall Kennedy, who is particularly concerned about the harmful impact of crack and other drugs on the black community and the fact that law enforcement has traditionally underserved minority communities. Kennedy states that "the most lethal danger facing African-Americans in their day-to-day lives is not white, racist officials of the state, but private, violent criminals (typically black) who attack those most vulnerable to them without regard to racial identity."[28] Kennedy contends, therefore, that what is needed is not less but more law enforcement in black communities.

While Kennedy's assessment of the historic relationship of law enforcement to the black community is well taken, his proposed remedy is rather narrow in scope. Law professor David Cole responds, "Jobs, housing, and education have also been inequitably distributed to the detriment of the African-American community. Their adequate provision would seem to be at least as likely to reduce crime as massive extended incarceration and without the negative effects on the community identified above."[29]

The issue of race and drug policy comes down to a question of choices. Yes, most police and prosecutors are not consciously racist in pursuing the drug war. Many firmly believe that they are aiding beleaguered communities caught in a vicious cycle of drug abuse and lack of opportunity. When a mother calls 911 to report a crack house in the neighborhood, it is only natural and proper for the police to respond swiftly.

But would more job and educational opportunities alleviate some of these neighborhood problems? Would more income support for low-income families be helpful? Before dismissing these notions as "hopelessly liberal" let us recall that these are exactly the tools used by middle-class communities to prevent these problems from developing or escalating.

The relatively recent development of drug courts, for example, demonstrates that practical innovations can both address problems in a constructive way and gain public acceptance. The drug court movement, originating in Miami and Oakland in the early 1990s, involves establishing specialized courts that hear only drug cases with the goal of diverting appropriate cases to treatment. Preliminary evaluations of these programs demonstrate that addicts who complete the treatment program are less likely to become engaged in drug use or crime than comparable offenders who do not go through the program.

The cost-effectiveness of a treatment approach to substance abuse has been demonstrated in a number of recent studies. A 1994 study conducted by the California Department of Alcohol and Drug Programs, for example, found that every dollar invested in substance abuse treatment generated seven dollars in savings, primarily through reductions in crime and reduced hospitalizations.[30] Similarly, the RAND Corporation analyzed the relative impact of harsher sentencing policies and expanded treatment on cocaine consumption. Their analysts concluded that spending $1 million to expand the use of mandatory sentencing to drug offenders would reduce consumption nationally by 13 kilograms, that arresting and incarcerating more dealers would reduce consumption by 27 kilograms, but that expanding treatment to more heavy drug users would result in a 100-kilogram reduction.[31]

These and similar programs are not difficult to implement. They also hold the potential for long-term cost savings and represent a more humane approach to the problem of substance abuse than mandatory sentencing and long-term incarceration. In recent years, such programs have been implemented successfully in many communities around the country. Despite this, the drug war becomes more entrenched each day.

NOTES

1. Barry Bearak, "Big Catch: Drug War's Little Fish," *Los Angeles Times*, May 6, 1990.
2. All figures on drug arrests in this chapter taken from data provided by the FBI to the author.
3. Substance Abuse and Mental Health Services Administration, *Preliminary Results from the 1996 Household Survey on Drug Abuse* (Washington, D.C.: Substance Abuse and Mental Health Services Administration, July 1997), p. 61.
4. Substance Abuse and Mental Health Services Administration, *National Household Survey on Drug Abuse, Population Estimates 1995* (Washington, D.C.: Substance Abuse and Mental Health Services Administration, June 1996), pp. 18–19.
5. Ibid., pp. 30–31.
6. Ibid., pp. 36–37.
7. James P. Lynch and William J. Sabol, "The Use of Coercive Social Control and Changes in the Race and Class Composition of U.S. Prison Populations," paper presented at the American Society of Criminology, Nov. 9, 1994.
8. Ibid., p. 30.
9. The SAMHSA surveys ask respondents if they have sold drugs, but most experts in the field do not consider these data nearly as reliable as the user figures.
10. Substance Abuse and Mental Health Services Administration, "Preliminary Results from the 1996 National Household Survey on Drug Abuse," (Washington, D.C.: Substance Abuse and Mental Health Services Administration, July 1997), Tables 314B and 315B.
11. John M. Hagedorn, "The Business of Drug Dealing in Milwaukee," Wisconsin Policy Research Institute, June 1998.
12. K. Jack Riley, *Crack, Powder Cocaine, and Heroin: Drug Purchase and Use Patterns in Six U.S. Cities*, National Institute of Justice, Dec. 1997, p. 1.
13. Patricia Davis and Pierre Thomas, "In Affluent Suburbs, Young Users and Sellers Abound," *Washington Post*, Dec. 14, 1997, p. A20.
14. Allen J. Beck and Darrell K. Gilliard, *Prisoners in 1994* (Washington, D.C.: Bureau of Justice Statistics, August 1995), p. 13.
15. Douglas C. McDonald and Kenneth E. Carlson, *Federal Sentencing in Transition, 1986–90* (Washington, D.C.: Bureau of Justice Statistics, June 1992), p. 4.
16. Christopher J. Mumola and Allen J. Beck, *Prisoners in 1996* (Washington, D.C.: Bureau of Justice Statistics, June 1997), p. 11.
17. William N. Brownsberger, *Profile of Anti-drug Law Enforcement in Urban Poverty Areas in Massachusetts*, Harvard Medical School, 1997, p. 21. The study also documented that Hispanics were 81 times more likely than whites to be incarcerated for a drug offense.

18. Randolph N. Stone, "The Criminal Justice System: Unfair and Ineffective," paper presented at the Chicago Assembly on "Crime and Community Safety," November 19–20, 1992, pp. 2–3.
19. Susan FitzGerald, "'Crack Baby' Fears May Have Been Overstated," *Washington Post Health*, Sept. 16, 1997.
20. United States Sentencing Commission, *Cocaine and Federal Sentencing Policy* (Washington, D.C.: United States Sentencing Commission, February 1995), pp. 122–23.
21. United States Sentencing Commission, p. 172.
22. Dan Weikel, "War on Crack Targets Minorities over Whites," *Los Angeles Times*, May 21, 1995.
23. Miles D. Harer, "Do Guideline Sentences for Low-risk Traffickers Achieve Their Stated Purposes?" *Federal Sentencing Reporter* 7.1 (1994).
24. James P. Lynch and William J. Sabol, *Did Getting Tough on Crime Pay?* (Washington, D.C.: Urban Institute, 1997).
25. Ibid., p. 8.
26. Ibid., p. 7.
27. Angie Cannon and Jodi Enda, "Clinton: Cut Disparity in Cocaine Laws," *Philadelphia Inquirer*, July 23, 1997, p. A13.
28. Randall Kennedy, "The State, Criminal Law, and Racial Discrimination," *Harvard Law Review* 107 (April 1994), p. 1259.
29. David Cole, "The Paradox of Race and Crime: A Comment on Randall Kennedy's Politics of Distinction," *Georgetown Law Journal* 83 (Sept. 1995), pp. 2568–69.
30. State of California Department of Alcohol and Drug Programs, *Evaluating Recovery Services: The California Drug and Alcohol Treatment Assessment* (Sacramento, Calif.: State of California Department of Alcohol and Drug Programs, April 1994), p. 89.
31. Jonathan P. Caulkins, et al., *Mandatory Minimum Drug Sentences: Throwing Away the Key or the Taxpayers' Money?* (Santa Monica, California: RAND Corporation, 1997), pp. xvii–xviii.

9—What's Class Got to Do with It?

The trial of O. J. Simpson, however unusual, taught the nation much about media, celebrity, and the racial divide. The trial also highlighted the intersection of issues of race and class, and how these categories play out in the criminal justice system.

Regardless of where one stands on the question of Simpson's guilt or innocence, few persons doubt that had he been a low-income African American male, rather than a wealthy star, his criminal trial would have had a very different outcome. Even if one believes that a black man charged with killing two white people suffers no disadvantages in the court system, the burdens involved in a criminal trial became painfully clear in the Simpson court proceedings—and, clearly, ones that no indigent defendant, or even a defendant of limited means, could overcome. The way in which a wealthy defendant's resources could purchase DNA expert testimony, pursue investigative leads regarding police misconduct, and assemble an all-star defense team—all perfectly legitimate in our court system—clearly proved to be critical in presenting a strong case to the jury.

So, when we speak about race and the criminal justice system, we are often in fact also talking about class. How to untangle these overlapping effects is a complex problem, but one that is critical to understanding the status of African Americans and the criminal justice system.

The criminal justice system in general and prison in particular have long served as the principal arena for responding to the crimes of lower-income people. The demographics of the prison population illustrate this well: a 1991 survey of state inmates conducted by the Justice Department found that 65 percent of prisoners had not completed high school, 53 percent earned less than $10,000 in the year prior to their incarceration, and nearly one half were either unemployed or working only part-time prior to their arrest.

"So what?" many will say. "These prisoners have committed crimes, and many of them violent crimes—surely it is no surprise that they are now in prison." Perhaps not. But it is useful to consider what constellation of individual, family, and economic circumstances led to their incarceration.

Although drug offenses constitute the largest growth area of black incarceration, black males are also arrested and convicted quite disproportionately for committing violent crimes. African Americans accounted for 44 percent of those arrested for violent offenses in 1995, and an estimated 47 percent of the African Americans in prison in 1995 were incarcerated for a violent offense.

Clearly, the 44 percent black share of violent arrests is quite disproportionate to the 13 percent of the total population comprised of African Americans. How can we understand this high rate of black violent offending? To what extent is this a question of race—some would contend that this represents socialization issues or a "subculture of violence"—and to what extent is it a function of class, that is, the disproportionately low-income status of African American offenders?

In recent years, much new information has come to light on these issues through the insights provided by the National Youth Survey (NYS), a study of a sample of 1,725 youths aged 11-17 in 1976.[1] The survey has followed this cohort over a two decade period, using self-report analyses to track rates of offending behaviors. In particular, the NYS examines the extent to which members of the sample engage in serious violent offending, defined as aggravated assault (attacking someone with the idea of seriously hurting or killing the person), robbery (using force or strongarm methods to obtain money or other items from people), and rape (having or trying to have sex with someone against their will). The survey documents the age at which offenders first engage in serious violent offending as well the extent to which these behaviors continue through their teen years and twenties.

Delbert Elliott, former president of the American Society of Criminology, and his colleagues have analyzed the data from the survey in a series of analytical reports. The results are quite instructive and sobering in a number of regards. First, we find that engaging in violent behavior is quite prevalent across all demographic groups. Among males, 42 percent have engaged in some type of serious violent offending by age 27; 16 percent of females have done so as well.

Although these rates of involvement in violent behaviors are quite disturbing, the good news is that for most youth, these experiences are relatively brief in duration. The peak year of involvement in these offenses for males, for example, is 17; by age 24, the rate of participation is just half that of age 17. Similar trends can be seen for females as well.

In looking at rates of violent offending by race, we find a number of intriguing results. First, black males engage in serious violent offending at rates that are higher than white males, but not dramatically so.[2] By age 18, 40 percent of black males have reported at least one instance of offending, compared to 30 percent of white males. By age 27, the figures are 48 percent for black males and 38 percent for white males. Thus, by age 27, the ratio of blacks and whites who have *ever* engaged in violent offending is about 5:4. For lower-class males, the differences are even smaller, about 7:6. Looking at these figures, Delbert Elliott concludes that if this rate is considered "a crude indicator of some predisposition to violence, we find little difference in predisposition by race."[3]

Studies that have examined crime rates controlled for class often mirror this finding. A recent review of homicide victimizations, for example, finds that "at higher socioeconomic levels, blacks and whites experience similarly low rates of homicide."[4]

A study of neighborhoods in Columbus, Ohio, by Ohio State University sociologists fleshed out this issue in greater detail.[5] Columbus affords good opportunities for measuring the relative significance of race and social class on crime, since it contains both black and white neighborhoods that are "extremely disadvantaged" as measured by poverty rates, proportion of female-headed households, male joblessness, and occupational structures. The researchers found that violent crime rates were considerably higher in the neighborhoods of high disadvantage, regardless of race. Black rates were somewhat higher than white rates, but these differences were generally not statistically significant; the researchers concluded that "it is these differences in disadvantage that explain the overwhelming portion of the difference in crime, especially criminal violence, between white and African American communities."[6]

Although the differences in *offending* rates as measured by the NYS are relatively modest, there are in fact substantial differences between black and white *arrest* rates as measured by the FBI's Uniform Crime Reports. While the ratio of male adolescent arrest rates among blacks and whites for serious violent offenses is 4:1, the NYS survey data indicate only a 3:2 ratio of offending. It appears that the chances that a black male youth who commits a violent offense will be arrested are substantially greater than for a white offender. Observers have attempted to explain this disparity in a variety of ways, most of which have been discussed earlier in this volume. Whatever the actual mix of explanations for these large disparities, it appears that, at least among adolescents, black illegal behavior is more likely to lead to attention by the criminal justice system.

While there are no dramatic differences in the degree to which blacks and whites become involved in violent offending at some point, there are significant differences in *how long* these violent behaviors persist. The NYS data reveal that black males are nearly twice as likely as white males to continue committing violent offenses into their twenties and nearly four times as likely to be involved by their late twenties. As a consequence, offenses by African American males are more likely to result in imprisonment, since the risk of incarceration is greater for adult offenders than for juveniles.

In trying to interpret this phenomenon, we need to consider the dynamics of youthful offending. The primary reason why young offenders cease their criminal activities, whether they be occasional or frequent, is essentially because, as they reach their twenties, many of them get married, go to college, find jobs, and generally take on adult roles, which they come to find more rewarding than street life.

But, for large numbers of young black men, these more positive lifestyle options are limited or more difficult to attain. For this reason, the positive rewards of leading a mainstream lifestyle often appear too distant to outweigh the lure of street life. An analysis of the NYS data finds, for example, that among 18–20-year-old youth who are employed or living in a stable relationship with a spouse or partner, there are no significant differences in the persistence of offending by race, but that among black males who fail to attain this status, violent offending is more likely to continue. Thus, a key question becomes the degree of access to legitimate employment among males in their late teens and early twenties.

Street-level research with gang members in Milwaukee adds some dimension to these findings.[7] Researchers interviewed African American and Latino gang members, many of whom were involved in drug dealing over a period of time: they found that a small proportion of the individuals were committed to drug dealing as a career, but the majority "were not firmly committed to the drug economy."[8] In fact, most of the gang members had a surprisingly conventional lifestyle orientation. For many, drug dealing was not a full-time occupation but, rather, a means of earning extra income at times when their earnings from legitimate employment were down. The researchers also found that most of the gang members shared conventional aspirations about economic security and even conventional ethical beliefs about the immorality of drug dealing, although they justified their own drug sales as necessary for survival. Such research sheds light on the interplay between legitimate and illegitimate work, and on the degree to which greater economic opportunity might provide attractive options for at least some of these offenders.

It also challenges the prevailing notion that the lure of quick profits from the drug trade is so attractive as to render useless any attempts to encourage adolescents. The Milwaukee researchers found that, despite the fact that drug selling yielded a considerably higher hourly rate of income than low-skilled jobs, there was a shift toward legitimate work when it was available. This is in keeping with the previously discussed conventional values of the group.

Research on drug dealers in Washington, D.C., found a similar relationship between legitimate and illegitimate employment.[9] Of a sample of drug dealers who were identified through arrest records, nearly all of whom were African American, two thirds were employed at the time of arrest. They were generally working at low-wage jobs and earning a median income of $800 a month. Drug dealing for these young men essentially was a form of "moonlighting," a supplement to their legitimate employment, with daily sellers bringing in a median of $2000 a month in drug sales. When asked their opinion of various occupations, fully 82 percent of the drug sellers responded that they "did not at all admire" a person who sold drugs, a figure exceeded only by the occupation of pimp.

The Washington researchers also found that although dealers faced substantial risks in selling drugs—either through arrest or physical harm from rival dealers—"such risks failed to deter substantial numbers of young males from participating in the trade."[10] Given adolescents' lesser concern for physical harm and/or their future prospects, they conclude that "the prospects for raising actual and perceived risks enough to make for markedly more deterrence through heavier enforcement against sellers do not appear promising."[11]

These data appear to suggest that strategies designed to create economic opportunities for disadvantaged youth might benefit communities in two ways—first, by providing necessary income and job experience for youth and, second, by reducing the attractiveness of drug selling to make money. For those individuals who sell drugs to support their own addiction, of course, treatment programs are also a critical component of the necessary response.

Ethnographic research in three neighborhoods in New York further illustrates these needs. Researchers interviewed residents of different neighborhoods that included a primarily African American housing project, a Hispanic neighborhood bordering on a declining industrial area, and a white working-class community. They attempted to assess how each neighborhood responded to changing economic circumstances.

The researchers found that the white working class community coped with changing economic realities far better than did the minority neighborhoods, largely because whites enjoyed greater access to labor market opportunities. Summarizing this dynamic, one observer describes how white residents

> found personalized job referral networks that led adolescents to adult employment opportunities, with jobs circulating through friendship, family, and neighborhood-based connections that linked local residents to desirable blue-collar jobs throughout the metropolitan labor market. In contrast, the Hispanic and black neighborhoods . . . were more physically isolated from centers of employment. Many of the parents in these neighborhoods had no jobs, while those parents who were employed tended to work in government jobs that recruited by bureaucratic means rather than through personal contacts.[12]

Black youth are also more disadvantaged that white youth in the degree to which they suffer the concentrated effects of poverty. In other words, it is not necessarily poverty per se that is a primary determinant of a host of social ills; rather, it is concentrated poverty, such as is seen in many inner-city neighborhoods. Due to the long history and persistence of housing segregation in the United States, many black communities remain largely isolated. This is particularly the case in low-income black communities.

Census data underline the problem. While 70 percent of poor non-Hispanic whites lived in nonpoverty areas in the ten largest U.S. cities in 1980, only 16 percent of poor blacks did.[13] And, while less than 7 percent of poor whites lived in areas of extreme poverty, fully 38 percent of poor blacks lived in such neighborhoods. Inner-city residents simply do not have access to the contacts and opportunities normally available to others in society. This does not suggest that a job creation approach to these problems is sufficient, of course, since the interaction of family and community supports can also play a significant role in the behavioral outcomes of individuals. But jobs help.

Given the findings regarding the intersection between race and class, and the potential of using economic opportunity as a strategy for crime reduction, what has been the response of policy-makers? One recent series of events is quite telling. Early in President Clinton's first term in office, following the Los Angeles riots, he called attention to the nation's urban crisis. Many experts were recommending a $60 billion economic package to stimulate job creation and economic development. Assuming that the political climate at the time would not support such an expenditure, the administration instead proposed a $30 billion package. Caught up in deficit reduction fever, though, the House passed only a $16 billion bill, which was promptly killed by the Senate in favor of a $5 billion allocation for unemployment insurance and some other domestic programs. The rationale for the cuts was essentially that the federal government could no longer "throw money at problems."

Who would have benefitted the most from such a stimulus package? Clearly, those people who are both most victimized by crime and by limited economic opportunities—primarily low-income African American and Latino communities.

Just a year later, though, members of Congress apparently had second thoughts about such spending and determined that they could in fact allocate $30 billion to these communities. This time, though, the appropriation took the form of a massive crime bill loaded with 60 new death penalty offenses, $8 billion in prison construction, "three strikes" sentencing, and other provisions certain to escalate the prison population. Amidst these punitive allocations were modest funds for programs to prevent crime and to reduce violence against women.

The members of Congress did not state, of course, that the result of the legislation would be to incarcerate impoverished young black and Latino men. At current rates, though, we can expect that about two thirds of the prison cells constructed through this act will be filled by minorities. This is not exactly what neighborhood leaders had in mind when they called for targeted investments to help rebuild their beleaguered communities.

NOTES

1. Delbert S. Elliott, "Serious Violent Offenders: Onset, Developmental Course, and Termination — the American Society of Criminology 1993 Presidential Address," *Criminology* 32.1 (1994), pp. 1–21. All subsequent data on the NYS are taken from this source.
2. In all data, white does not include Hispanic.
3. Elliott, "Serious Violent Offenders," p. 8.
4. John Hagan and Ruth D. Peterson, "Criminal Inequality in America: Patterns and Consequences," in Hagan and Peterson, eds., *Crime and Inequality*, (Stanford, Calif.: Stanford University Press, 1995), p. 20.
5. Lauren J. Krivo and Ruth D. Peterson, "Extremely Disadvantaged Neighborhoods and Urban Crime," *Social Forces* 75 (Dec. 1996), pp. 619–50.
6. Ibid., p. 642.
7. John M. Hagedorn, "Homeboys, Dope Fiends, Legits, and New Jacks," *Criminology* 32.2 (1994), pp. 197–219.
8. Ibid., p. 207.
9. Peter Reuter, Robert MacCoun, and Patrick Murphy, "Money from Crime: A Study of the Economics of Drug Dealing in Washington, D.C.," (Santa Monica, Calif.: RAND Corporation, June 1990).
10. Ibid., p. xiii.
11. Ibid.
12. John Hagan, "The Class and Crime Controversy," in John Hagan, A. R. Gillis, and David Brownfield, eds., *Criminological Controversies: A Methodological Primer* (Boulder, Colo.: Westview Press, 1996), p. 12.
13. Robert J. Sampson and William Julius Wilson, "Toward a Theory of Race, Crime, and Urban Inequality," in Hagan and Peterson, *Crime and Inequality*, p. 41.

10 — "Give the Public What It Wants": Media Images and Crime Policy

The role of the media has been a critical factor in influencing the direction of crime policy in recent years. In assessing the role of the media, one needs to recognize first that "the media" is a complex set of competing interests. The term encompasses a broad spectrum that includes the *New York Times*, the *National Inquirer*, National Public Radio, MTV, and countless other outlets of information and entertainment. Nevertheless, in a variety of ways, media images and information have converged to shape public perceptions of crime, offenders, and incarceration policy in ways that are often misleading.

Such an assertion may appear counterintuitive to those who have studied recent media coverage on certain criminal justice issues. On mandatory sentencing, for example, media attention has been fairly critical. Editorials in recent years in all almost all major print media—the *New York Times*, *Washington Post*, *Los Angeles Times*, and many others—have been sharply critical of mandatory sentencing. A sympathetic cover story in the black magazine *Emerge* on Kemba Smith, a 24-year-old first-time offender who was sentenced to 24 years for her role as a drug "mule" for her boyfriend drug dealer, generated the largest reader response in the magazine's history.

Given this virtual onslaught of news and editorial coverage, one would almost think that mandatory sentencing laws would be a dying breed. But this is hardly the case. As sound as some of the coverage has been on this issue, it nonetheless operates within a broader media environment. Most images of the crime problem communicate fear, anxiety, and a distorted sense of the actual extent of the problem. This serves to overwhelm any intelligent or informative discussion of the issues.

Many have noted that the influence of print media is rapidly being eroded by electronic media, and by television in particular. Fewer people read newspapers or rely on them for their main source of news; television, on the other hand, with its seemingly endless supply of new channels, has become the primary medium for information. And its power lies in the images it presents on the screen.

The Center for Media and Public Affairs, a Washington-based media monitoring organization, publishes an annual survey of issues covered on the evening news by the three major television networks. In 1993, the center reported that crime stories on network television had doubled from the previous year, with murder stories tripling.[1] Overall, one out of every eight stories featured on the evening news was a crime story.

By 1995, the networks featured more than 2,500 crime stories on the evening news, a 52 percent increase over the previous high in 1993.[2] While reports on the O. J. Simpson trial accounted for a third of this total, overall coverage had risen dramatically even excluding this story. Murder stories (excluding the Simpson case), for example, rose by 336 percent from 80 stories in 1990 to 375 by 1995, a period in which *actual* murder rates had declined by 13 percent.

Network evening news broadcasts are significant as a source of information, but the most heavily watched news programs are the late local news shows. Here the images are even more provocative, not to mention often misleading: in virtually every city in the country, crime stories dominate this coverage. For example, a recent study of television reporting in Philadelphia found that crime news represented almost one third (31 percent) of the stories on the local evening news, and that three-quarters (76 percent) of the crime stories were featured in the first segment of the news shows (prior to the first commercial break).[3]

Part of the reason for this is that crime makes for good visual effects. A story on an actual crime is much more interesting to watch than a general report about crime rates. But the dominance of crime stories also reflects the way that news is gathered and reported, particularly at the local level.

New York Times reporter Steven Holmes contends that the proliferation of crime stories is related to the fact that local news is dominated by information generated by government institutions.[4] The five o'clock local news can focus on the activities of various government bodies—a city council, the mayor's office, or state legislative bodies. But since government essentially closes down at five o'clock, it can no longer generate fresh news for the eleven o'clock broadcast. The main government newsmaking agency that stays open late enough for breaking local news is the police department. Crime news is also popular with local news producers because it is relatively inexpensive to produce. Former NBC News President Lawrence Grossman describes how "the crime scene, marked off in yellow police tape, doesn't move; no matter when the reporter arrives there's always a picture to shoot, preferably live. No need to spend off-camera time digging, researching, or even thinking. Just get to the crime scene, get the wind blowing through your hair, and the rest will take care of itself."[5]

There has been a good deal of discussion in recent years about the effects of television violence on viewers. While there is mixed evidence on this relationship, a more critical issue concerns the impact that television news violence has on public— and policymaker—attitudes about crime.

Recent analysis explores this issue in some detail. The Berkeley Media Studies Group examined news content of a week of local news broadcasts on 26 stations throughout California.[6] The researchers found that violence was the single most frequent story topic featured and that more than one half (55 percent) of the stories on youth involved violence, while more than two-thirds (68 percent) of the stories on violence involved youth. This is in contrast to FBI data showing that juveniles represent less than 20 percent of arrests for violence; young people are portrayed as contributing far more to the problem of violence than they actually do. Even within the reporting of violence, the Berkeley analysts found that reporting was far more likely (84 percent) to be "episodic" (focused on events) rather than "thematic" (providing a context for the events). Thus, news stories generally presented individual violent crimes with little discussion of the role of guns, alcohol, or drugs in contributing to the events at hand.

Such distortions in the perception of crime are not unique to the United States, although they are likely most developed here. In looking at the relationship between fear of crime and actual risks of victimization, the conclusion of the international victimization surveys coordinated by the Dutch Ministry of Justice has been that there is a "lack of much relationship between anxiety and risks of street crime," and that much of the level of fear of street crime may be determined by specific "cultural" pressures such as media influences.[7]

The impact of media images can be quite powerful. Political scientists at UCLA conducted an experiment in which they had subjects view television newscasts of crime stories.[8] Some of the stories identified a perpetrator, and some did not. Even in instances in which no specific reference was made to a suspect, 42 percent of the viewers recalled having seen one. In two thirds of these cases, they recalled the suspect as being African American.

Although distorted television images of crime and violence are troubling enough, a different problem is created by the way that news and feature producers frame issues for discussion. Let me illustrate with a personal example.

In 1995, the Alabama Department of Corrections reinstituted the chain gang in its prison system. State officials, riding a wave of "get tough" sentiment and presumably eager for media attention, began chaining inmates together in leg irons and having them crush limestone while being guarded by shotgun-toting officers. One might have thought that U.S. society had evolved to the point where such a practice would be inherently viewed as uncivilized, but apparently not.

In the weeks following the inception of the chain gang, I received numerous calls from reporters and producers. Many were just looking for the best "visuals" for the story, but a few of the more conscientious ones asked if I could aid them by providing research on the "effectiveness" of chain gangs. No such research exists—humiliation and control, not effectiveness, have always been the goal of such policies.

The confusion did not end there. Next came the producers for the network morning shows and talk shows to set up debates on the issue. Typically, they had no shortage of articulate spokespersons ready to castigate the prison officials, but they had tremendous difficulty finding an advocate for chain gangs. Could I help, they inquired, in finding such an individual? While I had little interest in being of assistance in this regard, it also seemed to me that they were missing a more fundamental issue.

The problem here was that there are not two sides to this issue, at least not in any responsible sense. Reasonable people may differ on the value of imprisonment or even the death penalty, but no reputable scholar or criminal justice official would even dignify the concept of chain gangs through such a "debate." The producers understand this, of course, but they also understand that such theatrics make for good television.

Print media, too, have contributed to distorted representations of issues of crime and justice. A study that appeared in the *American Journal of Public Health* concluded that print media representations of deaths caused by tobacco, alcohol, and illicit drugs were very inconsistent with actual mortality rates for each of these substances. While 4 percent of mortality-related news text was devoted to tobacco in 1990, deaths attributed to tobacco constituted 19 percent of actual deaths that year. Conversely, while illicit drugs were only responsible for 1 percent of all deaths, they represented 16 percent of the print coverage.[9]

Another study on newspaper crime reports found that homicides constituted half of all such stories and that there was little relation between the number of murder stories and actual murder rates in the cities studied. Instead, space devoted to such coverage appeared to be less a function of the "supply" of crime and more the product of the "newshole" space allocated to it.[10]

Rather than just bemoan the manipulation of crime news, though, producers and consumers need to seize opportunities to correct poor coverage of these issues and to establish a new orientation for their news-gathering. One such effort was initiated by television station KVUE in Austin, Texas. Producers at the station had become concerned that their crime coverage was both excessive and sensationalist. In order to cut back on coverage that was not critical to the local viewing area, the station's producers developed guidelines for airing a crime story. Crime news now needs to meet one or more of the following criteria:

1. Does action need to be taken?
2. Is there an immediate threat to safety?
3. Is there a threat to children?
4. Does the crime have significant community impact?
5. Does the story lend itself to a crime-prevention effort?[11]

Shortly after developing the guidelines, the station's producers elected not to cover a triple homicide that took place in a small town thirty miles east of Austin. The murders involved three acquaintances who shot and killed each other after getting into a Saturday-night brawl spurred by drugs and alcohol. Normally, this would have been a "no-brainer" in the news business; but, tragic as the incident was, the producers viewed the murders as an isolated event that had little immediate relevance for the viewing area. The early success of these news guidelines at KVUE has led to a good deal of interest, and some local news outlets round the country have begun to follow suit.

In addition to reducing sensationalist coverage, crime news can be more responsibly undertaken when reportage provides a crime's social context. The Berkeley Media Studies Group suggests that one means of accomplishing this is to incorporate more data of crime and violence. In California, for example, there are several factors of note: more than half of all violent offenders are under the influence of drugs or alcohol at the time of their offense; handguns are the leading cause of death of children; and most homicides occur between people who know each other.[12] Reporters should investigate where weapons are obtained, how substance abuse contributes to an offense, and whether officials are taking any preventive actions using the particulars of local crime conditions.

NOTES

1. Ellen Edwards, "Networks Make Crime Top Story," *Washington Post*, March 3, 1994.
2. "Network News in the Nineties," *Media Monitor* (July–Aug. 1997), p. 2.
3. Danilo Yanich, "TV News, Crime and the City," paper presented at the annual meeting of the Urban Affairs Association, May 1995, pp. 6–7.
4. Steven Holmes, "Media, Politics, and Public Opinion," presented at the Campaign for an Effective Crime Policy conference, December 2, 1994, Arlington, Virginia.
5. Lawrence K. Grossman, "Why Local TV News Is so Awful," *Columbia Journalism Review* (Nov.–Dec. 1997), p. 21.
6. Lori Dorfman, et al., "Youth and Violence on Local Television News in California," *American Journal of Public Health* 87 (Aug. 1997), p. 1311–16.
7. Pat Mayhew and Jan J.M. van Dijk, *Criminal Victimisation in Eleven Industrialised Countries* (The Netherlands: Ministry of Justice, 1997), p. 6.
8. Franklin Gilliam, Jr., and Shanto Iyengar, "Prime Suspects: Script-based Reasoning About Race and Crime," paper presented at the Annual Meeting of the Western Political Science Association, March 1997.
9. Karen Frost, Erica Frank, and Edward Maibach, "Relative Risk in the News Media: A Quantification of Misrepresentation," *American Journal of Public Health* 87 (May 1997), pp. 842–45.
10. Mark Warr, "Public Perceptions and Reactions to Violent Offending and Victimization," in Albert J. Reiss, Jr., and Jeffrey A. Roth, eds., *Understanding and Preventing Violence*, vol. 4 (Washington, D.C.: National Academy Press, 1994), p. 30.
11. Joe Holley, "Should the Coverage Fit the Crime?" *Columbia Journalism Review* (May–June 1996), p. 28.
12. Dorfman, et al., "Youth and Violence," p. 1315.

11—Unintended Consequences

In July 1996, Andrew Sonner, the longtime prosecutor for Montgomery County, Maryland, just outside Washington, D.C., ignited a local controversy around county drug policy. Sonner announced that henceforth his office would prosecute fewer small-time drug offenders and, instead, would concentrate its resources on drug sellers who either engaged in violence, were repeat offenders, or operated in high-crime areas.

Sonner's proposal was immediately attacked by County Executive Douglas Duncan, a Democrat like Sonner, who charged that the "county has had a zero-tolerance policy for drugs for a long time, and we're not going to change that as long as I'm county executive."[1] A war of words and competing policy proposals ensued over the next several months. Sonner's fleshed-out strategy included diverting more lower-level offenders to drug courts or treatment; ultimately, both sides compromised.

Despite the heat and rhetoric, Sonner's call merely reflected the thinking of most criminal justice practitioners. His primary offense was in publicly announcing his policy and its rationale. Had he just implemented the strategy within his office, it is likely that there would have been little public scrutiny or discussion.

Given the fact that criminal justice resources are limited, Sonner was astute enough to recognize that a law enforcement emphasis on one area of criminal activity will inevitably result in less attention to other areas, and that public policy decisions generate both intended and unintended consequences. These are lessons rarely acknowledged in political discourse.

DISPLACEMENT OF
CRIMINAL JUSTICE RESOURCES

One of the primary areas in which we can see the tradeoffs in criminal justice policy is in the realm of drug law enforcement, where there is mounting evidence that the increased emphasis on apprehending drug offenders is harmful to overall crime control efforts.

Economists at Florida State University have examined shifts in policing in Illinois and Florida in order to assess the effects of displacement on law enforcement priorities—in other words, how police attention to one area of enforcement offsets resources in other areas. In Illinois, they found that a 47 percent increase in drug arrests from 1984 to 1989 coincided with a 22.5 percent decline in arrests for drunk driving. Since drunk driving arrests nationally fell by only 1 percent during this time, the researchers argue that much of the displacement of these arrests in Illinois may have been due to the stepped-up pace of drug arrests. Perhaps not coincidentally, the number of traffic fatalities in Illinois during this time rose at a far greater pace than the national average, by 4 percent compared to 0.8 percent nationally.[2]

The same research team found that in Florida the substantial increase in drug law enforcement in the 1980s appeared to result in reduced attention to property offenses, which rose during that period. The authors speculate that the increase in property offenses could have partly been the result of factors related to a reduced law enforcement focus. Offenders who committed property crimes on a regular basis were likely to be arrested less frequently. Thus, a burglar who averages one burglary a week and might "normally" be apprehended after 10 burglaries might commit 15 offenses before being caught.[3]

Displacement of criminal justice resources takes place at the level of sentencing and corrections policy as well. While overcrowded prisons have been the subject of much attention, probation and parole populations have also been rising substantially in recent years. From 1985 to 1995, while the prison population increased by 121 percent, the number of offenders on probation rose by 57 percent, and those on parole rose by 133 percent. The increases in the number of offenders on probation or parole have resulted in higher caseloads for those systems, often reaching well over 100 offenders per officer. Yet while probation and parole populations constitute about three fourths of all persons under criminal justice supervision, just over 10 percent of corrections spending is devoted to these areas. As resources have been directed into prisons, the system's problems have been compounded for two reasons: prisons are far more expensive to operate than community supervision programs like probation and parole; and as the prison system drains ever-more resources from other parts of the system, it creates a greater reliance on incarceration.

The practical impact of this spiral appears in the courtroom on the day of sentencing. A judge is confronted with a nonviolent offender who has a prior conviction. The offender could be sentenced to community supervision with requirements for restitution, community service and alcohol treatment, or could receive a two-year prison term. Knowing that the local probation department averages caseloads of 125, the judge may understandably be reluctant to impose a nonincarcerative sentence on the grounds that little effective supervision would be possible and that community safety might be compromised. So, the offender is sentenced to prison at far greater cost, thereby creating additional pressure to build even more prisons.

Spending on prisons also has repercussions beyond the criminal justice system, particularly at the level of state spending. As virtually every state has increased its share of tax dollars devoted to corrections, funding for higher education has either declined or failed to keep pace with need. In California, for example, the state's sweeping "three strikes and you're out" legislation has contributed to substantial shifts in spending allocations: more than 40,000 offenders have been sentenced under its provisions in its first four years of implementation.

Projections by the RAND Corporation prior to the implementation of the law estimated that when used to its full extent, the law would double the proportion of the state budget devoted to corrections, from 9 percent to 18 percent in just an eight-year period.[4] With state Medicaid costs also rising and minimum levels of K–12 spending required by law, the most likely place for funding cuts is the higher education budget.

The impact of these tradeoffs, both on a state's overall economy and on crime, may turn out to be quite dramatic, as described by University of California criminologist Joan Petersilia:

> Persons who fail to become educated in an ever more technologically sophisticated economy are being squeezed out and are unable to compete in a more competitive job market. They face higher unemployment rates and downward mobility, which, in turn, are associated with poverty, substance abuse, female-headed households, and homelessness—all factors related to increased crime.[5]

These tradeoffs are rarely discussed in the world of public policy. Legislators do not pass an appropriations bill that states that funding for new prisons will be taken from state colleges, nor are parents of state college students informed that tuition increases are due to budget cutbacks caused by increased prison spending. But these are often exactly the repercussions of many public policy decisions.

THE HIDDEN IMPACT OF INCARCERATION

The prison experience as a whole has a set of negative consequences for many of those who go through it. A particularly disturbing development related to large-scale incarceration in the 1990s is the rapid spread of tuberculosis and HIV infection among inmates.

In New York City, for example, a major multidrug-resistant form of tuberculosis emerged in 1989, with 80 percent of all cases being traced to jails and prisons.[6] By 1991, the Rikers Island jail had one of the highest TB rates in the nation. The deadly combination of jail overcrowding, inadequate ventilation, and an ill-prepared medical system contributed to rates of infection not seen in decades.

HIV prevalence among prisoners has similarly exploded in recent years, with the rate of infection nearly thirteen times that of the non-prison population.[7] The primary causal factor in this regard is the dramatic escalation in the incarceration of drug offenders, many of whom engage in intravenous drug use, share needles, and/or trade sex for drugs.

Because inmates as a group often have relatively marginal relationships to legitimate employment to begin with, a stay in prison can seriously affect one's future earnings prospects. One economist's study of the impact of imprisonment on future wages concluded that among a sample of youth incarcerated in 1979 there was a 25 percent reduction in the number of hours worked over the next eight years.[8] Some of this reduction was attributed to recidivism and subsequent incarceration, and some to the negative effects of incarceration, such as failure to attain relevant work experience.

The scale of current imprisonment rates may also undermine the deterrent value of incarceration. Certainly prison has some deterrent value—but what happens to that deterrent effect as the experience of prison becomes pervasive in some communities? Some criminologists speculate that the impact of deterrence is in part related to the "mystery" of the prison experience. "People imagine a harsh and forbidding environment in which brutal and victimizing experience is commonplace," writes Todd Clear, a professor at Florida State University. "They also imagine the shame and humiliation that follows others learning of their prison history."[9] As imprisonment becomes a more routine experience in many African American neighborhoods, that sense of shame may decline. This is not to suggest that prison does not fundamentally remain an experience of brutality or humiliation; rather, as people survive the experience, the forbidding nature of the institution may be lessened in the eyes of the larger community. In addition, increasing the number of lower-level offenders who are locked up may contribute to a lessening of respect for the justice system if it is perceived as a system that is unjustly expanding the use of imprisonment.

There are also a set of consequences for the families and communities of offenders which vary depending on the individual and the offense. Removal of a violent offender who routinely terrorizes a neighborhood brings some level of public safety to the community, and this is obviously desirable, even if the individual's family experiences a loss. But what about the removal of large numbers of property or drug offenders? Some modest reductions in crime may be achieved this way, but negative consequences often ensue as well.

The degree to which these effects are prevalent is very much a function of the demographics of the affected community as well. In most communities, the number of offenders sentenced to prison at any given moment will be relatively modest and, therefore, any impact on the community fabric is likely to be modest. But in communities where substantial numbers of people are incarcerated, particularly low-income African American neighborhoods, a certain threshold may be reached whereby the compounding effects of incarceration become quite substantial.

Within the African American community, the sheer number of adult males locked up now is quite staggering: as of 1995, 7 percent of all adult black males were incarcerated in a prison or jail on any given day. Due to the cycling of offenders in and out of the system, over a period of time, incarceration affects a substantially greater share of the population than is in prison or jail at any given moment.

One effect of these trends is to contribute to the declining number of marriageable men in the African American community. Along with high rates of homicide, AIDS-related deaths, and other factors, this has resulted in a substantial imbalance in the male–female ratio among African Americans. Whereas gender ratios for African Americans at birth are about 102-103 males for every 100 females compared to a ratio of 105-106 per 100 for whites, by ages 20-24 the black gender ratio is 97 and the white 105. In the age range 40-44 the black ratio declines to 86 and the white to 100.[10] Further, men who have been imprisoned or are likely to be often have very limited financial resources or potential, and are hardly strong marriage prospects.

Some might surmise that a lower number of males would lead to a lower crime rate, given that males account for a disproportionate share of crime; but, as health sciences professor David Courtwright argues, whatever gains are achieved by having fewer males in a community are offset by men having greater "sexual bargaining power and hence the likelihood of illegitimacy and single-parent families."[11] One analysis of census data from 171 cities finds that these gender ratios are a very strong predictor of family disruption, and goes on to suggest that this leads to a greater likelihood of violence.[12] Thus, family disruption increases crime, which leads to greater numbers of prisoners, which leads to more family disruption, and so on — a vicious cycle for all concerned.

Much of the impact of increasing incarceration on crime control also relates to what can be described as the informal mechanisms of control that exist in varying degrees in all communities. The formal mechanisms of police and courts provide some measure of public safety, but families, schools, religious bodies, and other institutions also serve to transmit values and promote positive role models. William Julius Wilson describes how crime and unemployment may be liked in many low-income communities through their impact on these mechanisms:

> Neighborhoods in which adults are able to interact in terms of obligations, expectations, and relationships are in a better position to supervise and control the activities and behavior of children. In neighborhoods with high levels of social organization, adults are empowered to act to improve the quality of neighborhood life — for example, by breaking up congregations of youths on street corners and by supervising the leisure activities of youngsters. Neighborhoods

plagued by high levels of joblessness are more likely to experience low levels of social organization: the two go hand in hand. High rates of joblessness trigger other neighborhood problems that undermine social organization, ranging from crime, gang violence, and drug trafficking to family breakups and problems in the organization of family life.[13]

The negative consequences of high incarceration rates in some communities may actually lead to increases in crime in those communities. For example, for children whose parents are imprisoned, feelings of shame, humiliation, and a loss of social status may result.[14] Children begin to act out in school or distrust authority figures, who represent the people who removed the parent from the home. Lowered economic circumstances in families experiencing imprisonment also lead to greater housing relocation, resulting in less cohesive neighborhoods. In far too many cases, these children come to represent the next generation of offenders.

The impact of rising incarceration on the next generation of children has been exacerbated in recent years by the growing number of women who are sentenced to prison. From 1980 to 1995, the number of women in prison increased by 417 percent, compared to a 235 percent increase for men. As we have seen, women are increasingly being locked up for drug offenses, also at greater rates than for men. As of 1991, one third of female state prison inmates were incarcerated for a drug offense, compared to one fifth of male inmates.

Three fourths of the women in prison in 1991 were mothers, and two thirds had children under the age of 18. Many of these women are single parents: their incarceration means their children are being cared for by grandparents or other relatives, or being placed in foster care. Altogether, an estimated 1.5 million children have parents in prison.

The effects of the incarceration of women on children were demonstrated in a nine-state survey conducted by the National Council on Crime and Delinquency.[15] Researchers found that over half the women inmates had never received a visit from their children since their admission to prison. The most common reason for this was the distance from the children's home to the prison, more than 100 miles on average.

The impact of the criminal justice system on communities goes beyond issues of economic well-being and family stabilization. It also includes issues of democratic participation and political influence. One of the most dramatic ways in which this emerges is voting rights. Almost all states have laws restricting the right to vote for convicted felons. Forty-six states deny the right to vote to anyone who is imprisoned, thirty-two restrict voting privileges of offenders on probation and/or parole, and in fourteen states anyone ever convicted of a felony can lose the right to vote for life. For example, an 18-year-old first offender convicted of writing a bad check in Florida or Virginia who successfully completes a sentence to probation loses the right to vote for life. The only means by which voting rights can be regained in such instances is through gubernatorial action, a cumbersome and bureaucratic process few offenders are able to negotiate.

A study conducted by The Sentencing Project and Human Rights Watch in 1998 concluded that an estimated 3.9 million Americans, or one in fifty adults, was either currently or permanently disenfranchised as a result of a felony conviction.[16] Of these, 1.4 million were African American males, representing 13 percent of all black men. In those states that impose disenfranchisement on ex-felons, the figures are truly enormous; one in four black men are permanently disenfranchised in Alabama, Florida, Iowa, Mississippi, New Mexico, Virginia, and Wyoming. Given that the current generation of children has a higher rate of contact with the criminal justice system, it is likely that as many as 30–40 percent of African American men will lose the right to vote for some or all of their adult lives. Thus, not only are criminal justice policies resulting in the disproportionate incarceration of African Americans; imprisonment itself reduces black political ability to influence these policies.

When the United States was founded, the franchise was restricted to a self-selected group of wealthy white men who excluded other groups such as women, blacks, felons, and the poor. After the Civil War and Reconstruction, restrictions were added, such as the poll tax and literacy requirements, specifically designed to disenfranchise blacks. Statutes were tailored to punish with disenfranchisement those offenses that blacks supposedly committed more frequently than whites. In South Carolina, for example, "among the disqualifying crimes were those to which [the Negro] was especially prone: thievery, adultery, arson, wife-beating, housebreaking, and attempted rape. Such crimes as murder and fighting, to which the white man was as disposed as the Negro, were significantly omitted from the list."[17]

Over time the poll tax, literacy requirements, and other restrictions have been erased—but not the exclusion of felons and ex-offenders. U.S. policies in regard to ex-offenders remain far out of line with international norms; no other democratic nation bars ex-offenders from voting for life or keeps such a significant proportion of its citizens from voting as a result of a felony conviction.

None of the preceding suggests, of course, that criminal behavior should be condoned or not have consequences. Indeed, removal of certain serious offenders from a community clearly has beneficial consequences for the community for the period of time that the offender is incarcerated. But any calculation of the impact of imprisonment that fails to take into account both the short-term and long-term consequences of massive incarceration is a deeply flawed analysis. Whether the objective is to produce community safety or a more inclusive society, the expansion of the prison system creates a more troubling set of consequences each day.

NOTES

1. Brian Mooar and Manuel Perez-Rivas, "Drug Policy Ignites Debate in Montgomery," *Washington Post*, July 4, 1996, p. A1.
2. Bruce L. Benson and David W. Rasmussen, *Illicit Drugs and Crime* (Oakland, Calif.: The Independent Institute, 1996), p. 32.

3. Bruce L. Benson and David W. Rasmussen, "Relationship Between Illicit Drug Enforcement Policy and Property Crimes," *Contemporary Policy Issues* 9 (Oct. 1991), pp. 106–114.

4. Peter Greenwood, et al., *California's New Three-strikes Law: Benefits, Costs, and Alternatives* (Santa Monica, Calif: RAND Corporation, 1994), p. 3.

5. Joan Petersilia, "Diverting Nonviolent Prisoners to Intermediate Sanctions: The Impact on California Prison Admissions and Corrections Costs," *Corrections Management Quarterly* 1.1 (1997), p. 14.

6. Paul Farmer, "Cruel and Unusual: Drug-Resistant Tuberculosis as Punishment," in Vivien Stern and Rachel Jones, eds., *Sentenced to Die? The Problem of TB in Prisons in East and Central Europe and Central Asia,* (London: Penal Reform International, 1999).

7. Dorothy E. Merianos, James W. Marquart, and Kelly Damphousse, "Examining HIV-Related Knowledge among Adults and Its Consequences for Institutionalized Populations," *Corrections Management Quarterly,* 1, 4 (1997), p. 85.

8. Richard B. Freeman, "The Labor Market," in James Q. Wilson and Joan Petersilia, *Crime* (San Francisco: ICS Press, 1995), p. 188.

9. Todd Clear, "Backfire: When Incarceration Increases Crime," in *The Unintended Consequences of Incarceration* (New York: Vera Institute of Justice, 1996), p. 10.

10. David T. Courtwright, "The Drug War's Hidden Toll," *Issues in Science and Technology* (Winter 1996–97), p. 73.

11. Ibid., p. 74.

12. Ibid., p. 77.

13. William Julius Wilson, *When Work Disappears* (New York: Knopf, 1996), pp. 20–21.

14. Clear, "Backfire," pp. 12–13.

15. Barbara Bloom and David Steinhart, *Why Punish the Children?* (San Francisco: National Council on Crime and Delinquency, 1993).

16. Jamie Fellner and Marc Mauer, "Losing the Vote: The Impact of Felony Disenfranchisement Laws in the United States," The Sentencing Project and Human Rights Watch; October 1998.

17. Andrew L. Shapiro, "Challenging Criminal Disenfranchisement Under the Voting Rights Act: A New Strategy," 103 *Yale L.J.,* (Nov. 1993), p. 540.

12—A New Direction for a New Century

In March 1998, a remarkable conference was held in Kingston, Canada. Titled "Beyond Prisons," the international symposium brought together 100 leaders of prison systems, nongovernmental organizations, and academia for several days of discussion of the idea that the "increased reliance on incarceration is not only unsustainable financially, but also largely ineffective in preventing future crime compared to other forms of intervention."[1] Participants came from nations as diverse as Brazil, England, New Zealand, and Zimbabwe to discuss approaches aimed at reducing the use of imprisonment throughout the world.

Perhaps most notable was the event's sponsor—the Correctional Service of Canada (CSC), the agency responsible for administering the Canadian prison system. This agency is in the forefront of encouraging international dialogue on a world "beyond prisons." Despite the many similarities and geographical proximity of Canada and the United States, the idea that such a conference would ever be sponsored by the U.S. Federal Bureau of Prisons, the counterpart to the Canadian CSC, is beyond even the realm of imagination.

There are those who contend that the United States is somehow different from other nations, and moreover, that the lesson of the 1990s is that prison "works." They argue that if crime rates have declined for much of the decade at a time when imprisonment rates have risen, there must be some relationship at work. Others suggest that the rise in incarceration has lowered crime rates, but that it has done so along with other factors—changes in policing, a less volatile drug trade, and demographic shifts.

What do we know in fact about whether prison has "worked" to control crime, and particularly the high levels of violence that plague the United States? Looking at trends from a handful of years in the 1990s is rather myopic, given the scale of the race to incarcerate over a quarter century. If we examine crime rates in the late 1990s compared to just prior to the inception of the prison rise in the early 1970s, about the best that can be said is that crime rates in *some* categories are *no worse* than they were when only one sixth as many inmates filled the nation's prisons. Thus, while murder rates have finally declined to their levels of twenty-five years ago, rates of reported violence (as measured by the FBI) are higher than at that time for rape, armed robbery, and aggravated assault. The alternative measure of crime, the Justice Department's victimization studies, indicates that violent crime neared a twenty-year high in 1994 before finally declining.[2] As previously noted, this decline coincided with changes in the drug trade, police success in disrupting the flow of guns to young people, and other factors. Overall, this experience would hardly seem cause for great celebration of the institution of the prison.

At the same time, the costs incurred through these policy changes have been dramatic, both in fiscal and human terms. The United States is now second only to Russia in the degree to which it imprisons its citizens, and the cost of the corrections system approaches $40 billion annually. Industrialized nations with lower rates of violence than the United States have not achieved this by incarcerating huge numbers of their citizens; they have maintained lower rates through regulation of firearms, lower levels of concentrated poverty, and other means.

The impact of imprisonment stretches beyond the 1.73 million people in the nation's prisons and jails at any moment. It is magnified by the several million more citizens who have passed through the gates in recent years, and by the millions of prisoners' families.

The toll that this has taken on the African American community, and increasingly the Latino community, is now truly staggering. Women of color are increasingly experiencing the combined impact of social and economic trends, as the confluence of poverty, substance abuse, prostitution, and incarceration envelopes larger numbers each year. One would think that such a state of affairs should give pause to those who smugly contend that prison "works." But thirty years of politically inspired rhetoric, willful ignorance of research and programmatic developments, and constrained policy options have conspired to make the United States choose the most punitive of responses.

Some would argue that current criminal justice policy is less narrow than this overview would suggest. Indeed, in recent years there has been an expansion of community policing efforts both in urban and rural areas. Various programs providing alternatives to incarceration have proliferated; they engage offenders in community service work, pay restitution to victims, and address educational and employment skills development. But despite the best efforts of many of these program personnel, the inexorable expansion of the prison system has continued.

It did not have to be this way. Imagine for a moment that we are back in 1985. There are now a half million inmates in the nation's prisons, 52 percent more than just five years previously. Policymakers have the opportunity to assess the status of crime, and in particular the national drug problem, along with the research evidence on effective solutions to these problems. Investments can be made in expanding prevention and treatment services and working with communities to develop locally based approaches to drug abuse and its attendant harms. By and large, none of this takes place; instead, a massive "war on drugs" ensues pouring unprecedented resources into law enforcement and incarceration. Ten years later, the number of drug offenders in prison has escalated by 605 percent, from 39,000 to 275,000, costing taxpayers more than $5 billion annually.

Despite all this, the war on drugs has not even been effective. In 1997, Barry McCaffrey, Director of the Office of National Drug Control Policy, reported that "if measured solely in terms of price and purity, cocaine, heroin, and marijuana prove to be more available than they were a decade ago.[3]

But effectiveness hardly seems to matter. When it comes to

thinking about crime, our national reflex is "punishment." The preventive and medically appropriate interventions we employ against illness are dismissed as "soft on crime"—as if any policymakers are in favor of crime.

There is a way out of the current malaise. First, we need to acknowledge the relatively limited role that incarceration, and the criminal justice system generally, plays in crime control. Most of us refrain from committing crimes each day not out of fear of a prison sentence but because we have better things to do with our lives. Families, communities, careers, and a sense of hope for the future work wonders to control crime in most instances.

For far too long, we have also created artificial barriers between victims and offenders. Who among us has not been victimized by crime? And who among us has led a life entirely without shame or an occasional foray into illegality? By pitting "victims' rights" against "prisoners' rights," we have done a disservice to all. A healthy society should do all it can to provide healing to those who have been harmed by crime while providing decent conditions to those who are imprisoned, the vast majority of whom will return to our communities someday.

Each day, these concepts are beginning to be recognized by those who labor in the fields of crime and victimization. The movement toward problem-solving policing that has emerged in the past decade is a refreshing sign that long-established traditions may need to be questioned for their relevance to a modern world. Increasingly, leaders in policing are now teaching us that since "we can't arrest our way out of the problem," we need new ways to conceptualize the problem of crime and to develop more pro-active responses.

Similarly, the burgeoning field of restorative justice offers hope that a new vision of coping with interpersonal conflict can inspire communities to reject a punitive orientation to problems. Through the mechanisms of victim–offender mediation programs, family group conferencing with juvenile offenders, and community-based sentencing boards, responsibility for act-ing upon interpersonal conflict is being taken on by the communities affected by these problems. Once the exclusive province of church-based reformers, these concepts and programs are now increasingly embraced by a broad spectrum of criminal justice officials and local communities.

There is a major constraint, of course, to the full flowering of a different approach to these problems, and that is a political establishment influenced by mass media who live in dread of any change of business as usual in crime control. One might hope that enough of this leadership would someday see the sweet light of reason and embark on a better course, but the nature of our institutions suggests that this will not happen on its own anytime soon.

Rather than looking for a political hero to lead us out of this wilderness, we would do better to consider how we might mobilize a greater constellation of forces to demand a more constructive approach. Some modest signs of such a movement are in sight.

The sheer cost of a massive prison system, while hardly the deterrent that some believed it might be, is nevertheless of concern to growing numbers of community leaders. As prisons drain resources from colleges and universities, leaders in higher education and the business community are beginning to question the societal implications of such transfers of resources.

With the war on drugs continuing to rage with little sign of success or cessation, growing numbers of citizens are questioning the relevance of a punitive approach to a public health problem. Within the criminal justice system, this had led to the expansion of drug courts and other diversionary programs that steer addicts into treatment. Contrary to political wisdom, this preventive approach is almost universally praised in the hundreds of communities in which it has been employed.

The minority communities that have historically borne the brunt of criminal justice policies have become more active in recent years both in the realm of crime policy and community development. We have seen this in areas ranging from criticism of federal drug laws for their disproportionate impact on low-income communities to the development of community-based programs for youth that provide mentoring and other services.

Weaving these disparate interests together to promote change is the challenge, of course. One can hope that there is enough commonality of purpose to find a unifying agenda. The drug policies that result in the massive incarceration of young people of color are not only harmful to minority communities, but they are an unwise investment of tax dollars for anyone— and everyone. Likewise, the diversion of resources from schools to the bricks and mortar of the prison system robs all of society of the full potential of our children.

Ultimately, we must decide what kind of society we hope to live in. We can try to comfort ourselves by calling prisons "correctional institutions," but it is clear that, after two centuries, we as a nation still cage the least fortunate among us to solve our problems.

NOTES

1. Ole Ingstrup, Commissioner, Correctional Service of Canada, personal communication, Nov. 11, 1997.
2. The two measures of crime show somewhat more conflicting trends in property offenses. The FBI reports indicate that despite recent declines, overall rates of property crime are higher than in the early 1970s; burglary is the only property offense that declined overall. The victimization studies show a steady decline in property offenses over a twenty-year period. As previously noted, the absence of drug crimes from both measures may mask the effects of any shift in offending from crimes such as burglary or robbery to drug selling.
3. Barry McCaffrey, *The National Drug Control Strategy* (Washington, D.C.: Office of National Drug Control Policy, 1997), p. 21.

Index